CONFLICT IN THE 20TH CENTURY

THE COLD WAR

Dr JOHN PIMLOTT AND IAN MATHER

FRANKLIN WATTS

London · New York · Toronto · Sydney

INTRODUCTION

The modern world is a very dangerous place. Since 1945 relations between the rival superpower blocs, led by the United States and Soviet Union respectively, have been very tense. The invention and refinement of nuclear weapons have made war a more frightening prospect. As the armed forces of East and West face each other in a number of "flashpoint" areas, it would take little to spark off a confrontation which could lead to the end of the world as we know it.

This volume offers an explanation of why this should be, charting the relationship between the superpowers since the heady days of Allied victory at the end of the Second World War. The period divides into three "phases". Between 1945 and the Cuban Missile Crisis of October 1962, when the world teetered on the brink of war, the relationship deteriorated into a frosty confrontation known as the Cold War. This reflected the deep differences of political, social and economic beliefs that existed between East and West. Both superpowers tried to expand their spheres of influence; both sides continued to develop nuclear weapons of awesome capability which did nothing to calm people's fears; both sides refused to accept that the motives of the other were anything less than threatening.

This was followed by a period of comparative calm, known as detente (1963-79), when both superpowers followed policies designed to prevent confrontation, but this did not last. Since 1979, the old tensions have re-emerged, producing a situation known as the "New Cold War".

We are still living in the latter period, with both sides mistrusting the other, vying for territorial control in key areas and remorselessly increasing their nuclear stockpiles. The future looks bleak, but if one looks back at the history of the last 40 years, there is some hope. As long as both sides remain fearful of the consequences of nuclear war, the world may yet survive. This volume is designed to provide that historical perspective.

DR JOHN PIMLOTT *Series Editor*

EDITORIAL PANEL

Series Editor:
Dr John Pimlott, Senior Lecturer in the Department of War Studies and International Affairs, RMA Sandhurst

Editorial Advisory Panel:
Brigadier General James L Collins Jr, US Army Chief of Military History 1970–82

General Sir John Hackett, former Commander-in-Chief of the British Army of the Rhine and Principal of King's College, London

Ian Hogg, retired Master Gunner of the Artillery and editor of *Jane's Infantry Weapons*

John Keegan, former Senior Lecturer in the Department of War Studies and International Affairs, RMA Sandhurst, now Defence Correspondent, *Daily Telegraph*

Professor Laurence Martin, Vice-Chancellor of the University of Newcastle-upon-Tyne

Europe divided: the Berlin Wall was built in 1961 to stop East Germans escaping to West Berlin. It has remained for well over 20 years symbolising the divide between East and West.

CONTENTS

Chapter 1   **The Superpower Divide, 1945-62**   6

Chapter 2   **Detente and the New Cold War**   22

Chapter 3   **The Nuclear Backcloth**   36

Chapter 4   **NATO and the Warsaw Pact**   42

Appendices
  Personalities   48
  East-West Flashpoints   50
  East-West Balance of Forces   52
  Spies and Spying   54
  The Space Race   56
  Chronology   58

Index   60

Glossary   62

THE COLD WAR IN EUROPE, 1945-86

- Warsaw Pact members
- NATO members
- Neutral countries
- Communist/neutral countries

CHAPTER 1
THE SUPERPOWER DIVIDE 1945-1962

Between 1941 and 1945 the United States of America and the Soviet Union were allies, working together to defeat Nazi Germany. However, within months of Germany's surrender on 8 May 1945, they were at loggerheads. Deep divisions opened up between the Soviet Union on the one hand and the United States and her allies on the other. Europe split into two opposing military blocs: as Winston Churchill, Britain's wartime prime minister, put it in March 1946, "an Iron Curtain has descended upon the Continent".

The Second World War produced devastation on an unprecedented scale. The toll in human lives is estimated to have been about 50 million, of which some 20 million were Soviet, 5 million German, 1.6 million Japanese, 397,000 British and 300,000 American. Many of the survivors were left without food or shelter and hundreds of thousands faced the future as refugees, unwilling or unable to re-turn to their pre-war homes. Entire cities had been reduced to rubble by mass bombing or the effects of battle, while Japan had experienced the full horror of atomic attacks. Once the war was over, the need for massive reconstruction, in human as well as material terms, was top priority.

Denazification

To begin with, the victorious Allies had one aim in common: to prevent a return of fascism – the ruthless form of government exemplified by the Nazis – parti-cularly in Germany. Their methods varied – in areas occupied by the British and Americans, a careful policy of "denazification" was initiated, whereby all people who had been active in Adolf Hitler's regime were removed from public office, while in Soviet-controlled areas, all Nazi officials were imprisoned and many of them shot – but the idea was to free Europe from the scourge of Nazism, exposing its crimes and ensuring that future generations were made aware of its evil.

In the Western areas, school children were told of the horrors of the concentration camps – indeed, in some regions the local people were forced to bury the emaciated bodies of the victims, often in the full glare of newsreel publicity – and special trials were carried out to find and punish the guilty men (and women) of the Nazi era.

Between November 1945 and October 1946, the more notorious Nazi leaders, including Hitler's henchmen Hermann Goering and Rudolf Hess, were brought to justice at Nuremberg; 12 of them were sentenced to death for crimes against humanity, and many more received long prison sentences. Other trials took place elsewhere, dealing with specific atrocities such as the massacre of American prisoners of war at Malmédy in December 1944, and similar justice was meted out to Japanese military leaders captured in August and September 1945.

The Yalta deal

But this was about as far as Allied co-operation went, for it was soon obvious that fundamental differences existed over the future of Europe. Some of these were already emerging towards the end of the war, when the three major wartime Allies – the United States, Great Britain and the Soviet Union – met at Yalta in February 1945. There the "Big Three" leaders, Franklin Roosevelt, Winston Churchill and Josef Stalin, made a "deal" involving concessions by the West which would prove to be crucial to the post-war world.

Stalin's main aim was to protect the Soviet Union from future attacks from the west (something that had already happened in both 1914 and 1941) by creating a "buffer zone", using the territory of western neighbours as the first line of defence. His ideal solution was a larger Poland, ruled by a government friendly to the Soviet Union. Stalin therefore proposed that Poland's western border should be moved, taking over German territory up to the Oder and Neisse rivers, and with the Soviet Union receiving part of eastern Poland. A Polish government of communists and non-communists would be allowed to take office in Warsaw.

Nazi leaders on trial at Nuremberg in November 1945; Hermann Goering is seated far left, middle row.

Churchill, Roosevelt and Stalin at Yalta, 1945.

The Western Allies agreed to this in exchange for a Soviet promise to enter the war against Japan two months after a German surrender. Many reasons for this fateful agreement have been suggested. It is known, for example, that Roosevelt was very ill (he died in April) and that he believed he could keep Stalin under control, while both Roosevelt and Churchill were desperate to ensure a Soviet declaration of war on Japan. In reality there was little anyone could do to stop the Soviets. By the beginning of 1945, Soviet troops already controlled Poland and by the end of the war a few weeks later, they had advanced as far as the Elbe, well to the west of the Oder-Neisse line.

Germany divided

Stalin also made other demands. He was firmly in favour of extracting financial "reparations" (compensation) from Germany to help pay for the enormous damage inflicted on his country during four years of bitter war. He demanded the equivalent of 20 billion US dollars as well as the right to strip Germany of her industrial and mineral assets and to use her people to rebuild Soviet economic strength. In order to gain control over German territory so that this could be carried out, Stalin readily agreed to the division of Germany into four zones, administered by the occupying armies of the United States, Great Britain, France and the Soviet Union respectively, with a similar split in the city of Berlin. Austria was to be occupied in much the same way, with Vienna under four-power control.

Final arrangements along these lines should have been made at the last of the wartime conferences, held at Potsdam (a suburb of Berlin) in July 1945, but by then circumstances had changed. Roosevelt was dead and had been replaced by his vice-president, Harry Truman. The results of a British general election, announced while the conference was in session, meant that Churchill was replaced by the leader of the new Labour (socialist) government, Clement Attlee. Both newcomers were convinced that too much had already been given away to Stalin and were determined to alter the agreements. But it was already too late. Stalin had begun to pave the way for a communist takeover of Poland and was prepared to offer no concessions over the future of Germany.

At Potsdam, the Allies did agree that Germany should be run by a Control Council made up of the commanders of the four occupying armies, with free elections being held as soon as possible to create a new German government. However, fundamental differences of opinion about the future of Germany soon emerged. The Western Allies wanted to rebuild Germany as a self-sufficient country, and did not want the expense involved in administering a shattered enemy state indefinitely. The Soviets, on the other hand, were still determined to exact heavy reparations from Germany, even to the extent of demanding some of this from the Western sectors.

This deepening rift ensured that no formal peace treaty with Germany could be signed – even today, such a treaty does not exist. Although some of the earlier agreements were carried out, most notably the Soviet declaration of war on Japan on 8 August 1945, the wartime relationship between the Allies had been soured. What was to become known as the "Cold War" had begun.

The Cold War

A "Cold War" is a state of hostility between rival countries that stops short of actual fighting. Instead conflict takes the form of propaganda, economic measures and a general policy of non co-operation. There were many reasons for the post-1945 Cold War. Underpinning them all were the fundamentally opposed political beliefs of the Western Allies and the Soviet Union, for although all had come together to defeat the common enemy of fascism, their world views were so different that rivalry was inevitable.

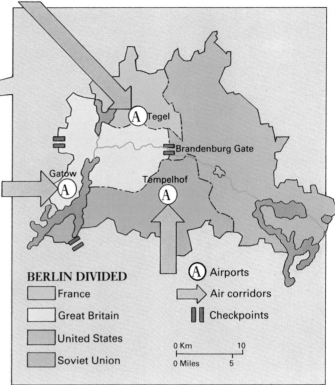

A DIVIDED GERMANY:
THE OCCUPYING POWERS, 1945-55

To the West, the ideal political system was one based on elections to a multi-party, democratic parliament, with economic policies determined by the free-market enterprise of capitalism, in which people were able to enjoy the fruits of their own labours. Such a system would, it was believed, allow the people to live their own lives and to enjoy certain basic freedoms such as those of political and religious belief.

By comparison, the Soviet system was controlled by the ideals of communism, in which the needs of the individual were subordinated to those of the society as a whole. Although the aim of a classless society in which the profits of labour would be shared between the people as required sounded fine in theory, the Soviets had been forced to impose strong central control on the economy and society in an attempt to put it into practice. In Western eyes, this destroyed the freedom of the individual; to the Soviets, it was a much fairer and less chaotic state of affairs.

Moreover, since the revolution of 1917, which had brought the communists to power in Russia, a declared aim of the communists had been to spread their ideas to other countries, and although Stalin officially

rejected this in the 1930s, aware that he faced enough problems in the Soviet Union without taking on the rest of the world, a general fear of Soviet expansion soon took hold in the West.

This was made worse by the events of 1945, for despite victory over the Germans there was little sign that the Soviets were prepared to withdraw behind their pre-war borders. The Soviet armies in eastern Europe were not reduced in size and, more significantly, the countries occupied by the Soviets in the final months of the war were not allowed to hold free elections or to adopt Western-style governments.

To many in the West, communism seemed to be gaining ground, and this view of Soviet motives cannot be ignored when trying to understand the Cold War. To the West, the Soviets were merely pausing before extending their rule over the rest of Europe; to the Soviets, the need for a buffer zone to protect their homeland was the overwhelming concern, justifying their policy of creating communist governments throughout eastern Europe. Add to this the Soviets' fear of American atomic weapons – which they could not even begin to match until 1949 – and the un-doubted personality clashes between leaders such as Truman and Stalin, who found it virtually impossible to talk calmly, and a pattern of reasons for the Cold War begins to emerge.

Soviet expansion

These reasons are best illustrated by reference to the events of 1945-62. Viewed through Truman's eyes, the world in 1945-46 seemed a very threatening place. When he took over as president of the United States in April 1945, most of eastern Europe – Bulgaria, Romania, Poland, Czechoslovakia, Hungary and parts of Austria and Germany – was already under Soviet military control. Stalin soon made it clear that he was prepared to impose permanent communist governments on the areas under his control, even if this required blatantly undemocratic methods.

Communist governments had also been set up in Albania and Yugoslavia, and in Greece communist and royalist factions had been embroiled in a civil war since October 1944. Finally, in China the communist forces of Mao Tse-tung – no different in most American eyes from the forces of Stalin's Russia – were beginning to achieve military success against the pro-Western Nationalists. It looked as if communism was extending its grip on key areas of the world.

The situation worsened when, on 24 February 1947, Britain announced that it could no longer afford to pay for military aid to the Greek royalists nor continue to help Turkey, a neighbour of the Soviet Union under pressure from Stalin to allow the establishment of Soviet bases on her soil. Britain's plight triggered Truman into launching a world-wide crusade against communism known as the Truman Doctrine.

On 12 March 1947, Truman outlined his policies to the United States Congress, arguing that the world faced a stark choice between two political philosophies. He said "one way of life is based upon the will of the majority, and is distinguished by free institutions, representative government, free elections, guarantees of individual liberty, freedom of speech and religion and freedom from political repression. The second way of life is based upon the will of a minority forcibly imposed upon the majority. It relies upon terror and oppression, a controlled press and radio, fixed elections and the suppression of personal freedom."

Congress, despite some opposition from liberals, radicals and even from some conservatives, approved Truman's commitment to confront the communist challenge wherever it appeared. Funds were approved for Greece and Turkey. The result was a general policy known as "containment", designed to prevent the spread of communism beyond its existing boundaries by offering military and economic aid to those countries under threat.

"Free Pass for the Marshall Plan",
a propaganda poster.

The Marshall Plan

This was followed by the unveiling of a broad strategy to keep western Europe out of communist hands, known as the Marshall Plan after General George Marshall, Truman's Secretary of State who originally suggested it. On 5 June 1947, Marshall proposed massive US economic aid to Europe to "permit the emergence of political and social conditions in which free institutions can exist." To the hard-pressed Europeans, it was too good to resist and they lost no time in agreeing.

Even the Soviets, ravaged by war, expressed an interest, applying for a six billion dollar loan from the Americans. But there were strings attached, for the Americans expected the receiving countries not only to adopt liberal democratic political ideas but also to use the money to buy American goods. As soon as this became apparent, the Soviets walked out of the negotiations in Paris (12 July 1947), taking the east Europeans with them.

Nevertheless, 16 countries took advantage of Marshall Aid, receiving a total of 72.5 billion dollars by December 1959. The money played a vital part in the post-war economic recovery of western Europe, but funds were also used by the US to interfere in the internal politics of France and Italy, both of which had strong communist parties. After 1950 two-thirds of the money was devoted to military purposes.

The Soviet bloc

The result was that the "Iron Curtain" dividing the capitalist west from communist eastern Europe became even more of a reality. Stalin reacted by forcing the communist bloc into a tighter grouping, the Communist Information Bureau (Cominform), and setting up a communist "common market", or economic union, known as the Council for Mutual Economic Assistance (Comecon), in 1949 with the aim of fostering economic development based on loans from the Soviet Union.

Stalin, who dominated the Soviet system at home, controlling the party machine and ruthlessly eliminating his rivals, was determined to establish a firm control over the so-called "satellite states" of eastern Europe. This policy came to a head in Czechoslovakia, a country which had enjoyed a brief period of democracy under elected communist governments immediately after the Second World War. Soviet influence had been felt, not least in pressures upon the Czechs to reject Marshall Aid. But elections were held in February 1948 which the non-communists seemed sure to win.

To prevent defeat, the communists, aided by the Soviets, seized political power before the election results could be announced. Non-communist ministers were arrested and one of the most prominent, Jan Masaryk, was found dead beneath his office window. The official verdict was suicide, but state archives, opened later, show that he was murdered. By March 1948, Czechoslovakia was firmly in communist hands.

But Stalin did not have things all his own way. At the same time as the Czechoslovak coup, he tried to impose his authority on Yugoslavia, a country already ruled by communists under the wartime guerrilla leader Tito (Josip Broz). Since 1945, Tito had insisted on taking an independent line, defying the Soviets, and when in March 1948 Stalin withdrew technical aid in an effort to control the Yugoslavs, Tito called his bluff.

Because of the practical difficulties of sending Soviet forces to Yugoslavia and the chances of confrontation with the West over any attempted invasion, Stalin had to back down. Up to the present day, Yugoslavia has been able to maintain an independent foreign and economic policy while still embracing communism.

Czech communists demonstrate in favour of "world peace" during a period of tense East-West relations, 1949.

Children watch as a C-54 Skymaster carrying essential supplies sweeps low over West Berlin, 1948.

The Berlin airlift

But Stalin did not stop there, for in June 1948 he provoked a deliberate crisis over Berlin, probably in an attempt to test the resolve of the West in its policy of anti-communism. The former capital of Nazism, situated more than 100 km (60 miles) inside east Germany and surrounded by Soviet-controlled territory, had been divided into four sectors in 1945, each to be occupied by the army of one of the victorious wartime allies.

Access to the city from the west was restricted to a single motorway, a railway, a network of canals and a carefully defined air corridor. By the time the Western Allies had gained Soviet permission to occupy their sectors in July 1945, the people of Berlin had already endured over two months of ruthless Soviet occupation. Those in the Western sectors therefore welcomed the arrival of their new rulers. Instead of demanding reparations, the American, British and French authorities in the *Kommandatura* (occupying authority) introduced policies of recovery and aid as they had in western Germany.

These culminated in June 1948 in the introduction of a new and stable currency, the Deutschmark. The resulting flow of funds from eastern to western sectors threatened to undermine Soviet attempts to impose economic control. The Soviets withdrew from the *Kommandatura* and, in an extremely provocative move, informed the West that the motorway into Berlin was closed "for repairs". Soon afterwards, the railway link was also closed and the use of the canals restricted. Berlin was cut off from the West.

The implication was clear: the Soviets were trying to force the Western allies to abandon Berlin. But the West refused to be intimidated and turned to the still open air corridor as a means of supplying the 2½ million inhabitants of West Berlin. On 26 June 1948 the Americans and British began an airlift of vital supplies and a crisis quickly developed. As aircraft followed aircraft into and out of the Western sectors, the Soviets responded by pouring troops into east Germany. Tensions rose even higher when three groups of American strategic atomic bombers were flown openly to bases in Britain. The chances of a major war developing increased daily, hinging on the degree of Western determination and whether the

Soviets would allow the airlift to continue.

In the event, the Soviets proved unwilling to take the risk, and despite further intimidation – including the use of fighter aircraft to "buzz" the Western transports – they held back from the awesome decision to close the air corridor, hoping no doubt that the high cost of the airlift would force the West to stand down. But the West regarded the crisis as a test of resolve and even when major difficulties arose, particularly in the winter months, they maintained the flow of supplies.

Their efforts saved West Berlin. Despite desperate shortages of fuel and electricity, a total of 2,323,000 tonnes of food and supplies, delivered by 195,530 aircraft flights over a period of 318 days, kept the Berliners alive, At times, aircraft were landing every few minutes and Gatow airport (see map on page 9) was said to be the busiest airport in the world, handling an average of 540 movements a day throughout the period of the airlift. Allied aircraft also flew out Berlin's exports, as well as undernourished children and people who needed medical treatment. By 12 May 1949, Stalin was forced to admit defeat and lift the blockade, although the airlift was to continue until late September as stockpiles of supplies were built up.

The creation of NATO

The Berlin crisis led to a permanent division of Germany. The Western powers, true to their policy of handing power back to non-Nazi politicians, created the German Federal Republic (West Germany) in May 1949 and the Soviets responded by forming their zone into the German Democratic Republic (East Germany) five months later. By then, two further developments had taken place which ensured the creation of potentially dangerous rival camps in Europe, between which the process of the Cold War was played out.

The first of these was the creation by the West of the North Atlantic Treaty Organisation (NATO). This had its origins in treaties between Britain and France in 1947 (the Treaty of Dunkirk) and between Britain, France, Belgium, the Netherlands and Luxembourg a year later (the Treaty of Brussels), in which the various parties agreed to help each other in the event of war. NATO itself came into existence on 4 April 1949, while the Berlin crisis was still going on, and involved a total of 12 member states – Belgium, Britain, Canada, Denmark, France, Iceland, Italy, Luxembourg, the Netherlands, Norway, Portugal and the United States.

The core of the Treaty was contained in Article 5, which stated that an attack upon any member country would be viewed as an attack against them all and reacted to accordingly. A joint military command was set up and, significantly, it was headed by a US general: the United States – departing from its normally isolationist policies – was formally committed to going to war in Europe in the event of Soviet aggression.

The birth of NATO: representatives of the 12 founder member countries sign the treaty in April 1949.

This was a crucial development in the Cold War, highlighting the growing awareness of Soviet policies that existed in the United States, but there was more to it than that. Fears of Soviet intentions increased, giving rise to a sense of paranoia, fuelled by a number of spying scandals. Two Americans, Julius and Ethel Rosenberg, were found guilty of passing secret information to the Soviets and executed as traitors, and Dr Klaus Fuchs, a German-born nuclear physicist living in Britain, confessed to spying activities.

Fears of the Soviets were translated into general hysteria about communism and other left-wing beliefs in the United States, and when Senator Joseph McCarthy instigated a Senate inquiry under his chairmanship, a virtual witch-hunt ensued. Some 3,000 US citizens were called to appear before the Senate subcommittee on "Un-American Activities" and many more were forced out of their jobs in government service, education and even entertainment when they were accused of less than right-wing views.

The situation was made worse by another important development of the late 1940s – the sudden Soviet test-explosion of an atomic device in 1949. Although the Soviets lacked the ability to drop such a bomb onto American soil, the fact that they had "caught up" so quickly with the Americans (who had been hoping to maintain a monopoly of such weapons) increased public disquiet.

This was further fuelled by government propaganda, determined to paint the blackest picture of the Soviet Union. Radio broadcasts from stations such as the Voice of America and Radio Free Europe spread this view worldwide, leading to Soviet moves to jam the air waves and to spread counter-propaganda.

Beyond Europe

In such circumstances, many Americans began to see the spread of communism as an integrated campaign designed specifically to undermine the interests of the United States. Nor was this an entirely unreasonable view. In October 1949, China fell to the communists under Mao Tse-tung – an event which immediately led to Soviet calls for the Nationalist Chinese to step down from their place in the Security Council of the United Nations and to an American veto of such a proposal – and in June 1950 the communist North Koreans, with Soviet backing, invaded pro-American South Korea, clearly intent upon expansion.

Senator Joseph McCarthy during the hearings of the Un-American Activities subcommittee in 1950. He was later discredited.

Korean refugees flee from the fighting, 1950.

In the latter case, the Americans were able to mobilise "Free World" opinion (and forces) to fight the aggression in a war that was to last for three years in Korea, but this was not the full extent of the problem. Elsewhere in the Far East, various Western or Western-backed countries were fighting against communist uprisings – the French in Indochina, the British in Malaya and the Filipinos in their home islands. The Americans did all they could to help, short of actually putting troops on the ground. Money and military equipment were made available to government forces and the idea of "containment" was extended. The United States had already used its influence in Latin America to form the Organisation of American States (1948) and NATO was protecting western Europe. They now formed other alliances to complete the encirclement of the communist bloc.

The details were left to John Foster Dulles, Secretary of State to President Dwight Eisenhower, elected to replace Truman in 1952. In September 1954, Dulles created an "Asian NATO" when the United States, Britain, France, Australia, New Zealand, Thailand, Pakistan and the Philippines came together to form the South East Asia Treaty Organisation (SEATO), and in 1955 the "wall" of containment was completed when Britain, Turkey, Iraq and Pakistan signed the Baghdad Pact, designed to keep the Soviets out of the Middle East. The latter had to be renamed the Central Treaty Organisation (CENTO) in 1959 when Iraq refused to agree to the inclusion of Iran, but the basic intention did not alter. By then, however, the situation in Europe had begun to change.

Death of Stalin

On 5 March 1953, Stalin died, bringing to an end an era in which the Soviet Union had emerged as a potential "superpower" (a country of immense power and prestige), capable of challenging the United States for world influence. But the cost had been high, and Stalin's successors, aware of the weaknesses of their country as it recovered from the ravages of four years of total war, began to move away from a policy of confrontation. In 1955 Nikita Khrushchev, a blustering, argumentative man, emerged as the new First Secretary of the Soviet Communist Party and, unlike Stalin, he proved willing to talk to the Western powers.

In February 1955, he offered to withdraw Soviet troops from Austria if the West would do the same and Austria became a neutral state; three months later, the Austrian State Treaty achieved just such an outcome. In July, in a new spirit of hope, Khrushchev met Eisenhower, together with the leaders of Britain and France, in Geneva for the first "summit meeting" since Potsdam. Although nothing dramatic was decided, an easing of tension seemed to be on the cards, particularly when, a few months later, Khrushchev openly attacked the policies of Stalin, describing him as a tyrant, and declared that "peaceful co-existence" between East and West was desirable.

But the Cold War could not be finished quite so simply, and both sides continued to feel threatened by the actions of the other. In May 1955, for example, the Western Allies decided to recognise the existence of West Germany by ending the occupation and allowing controlled rearmament within the context of NATO. By then, the NATO alliance had already been expanded by the addition of Greece and Turkey (in 1952), but this latest move could only help to provoke the Soviets – after all, it was still only 10 years since the end of the "Great Patriotic War", as they called the Second World War, in which 20 million Russians had died, and the Western countries were already rearming the Germans.

In response, the Soviets sought their own security agreement, designed to ensure their unquestioned military control of the satellite states of eastern Europe. On 14 May 1955, the day before West Germany became a NATO member, the Warsaw Pact was signed between Albania, Bulgaria, Czechoslovakia, Hungary, Poland, Romania and the Soviet Union, with East Germany as an official "observer" (she joined before the end of the year). Europe was now firmly divided into two armed camps.

The invasion of Hungary

To the Soviets, the Warsaw Pact was a perfectly justifiable counter to NATO, but the West took a different view, particularly when the Soviets used it to enforce their policies in the member states. East European countries had already suffered the experience of Soviet troops maintaining communist "solidarity" when, in June 1953, T-34 tanks had been used in East Germany to put down a workers' strike, called in opposition to food shortages and religious persecution.

However, this was nothing compared to events in Hungary three years later. In July 1956 students, intellectuals, workers and peasants demanded the removal of Hungary's Stalin-like leader, Matyas Rakosi, and the return of the more moderate politician, Imre Nagy. The crisis came to a head in October when police opened fire on a student demonstration in Budapest, and suddenly the whole country was up in arms. The army joined the uprising and at first the Soviets seemed prepared to compromise, recalling Nagy and allowing a measure of political and religious freedom.

Disabled Soviet tank, Budapest, 1956.

Stalin's head is knocked down in Hungary, 1956.

But the jubilation was short-lived. On 1 November, as Western attention was diverted to a crisis in Egypt, the politburo, or ruling body, in Moscow voted to invade Hungary, where Nagy had just announced his intention to leave the Warsaw Pact. On 4 November, the Soviet Army entered Hungary in force and tanks patrolled the streets of the major towns and cities. The Hungarian patriots fought back with what they had – in many cases little more than Molotov cocktails (petrol bombs) and rifles.

The outcome was inevitable. Within a very few days, the Soviets had re-established control, rounding up thousands of dissidents, executing Nagy and installing a "safe" communist leader, Janos Kadar, in his place. By then, a similar uprising in Poland had been nipped in the bud, fortunately without the need for tanks on the streets, and Wladyslaw Gomulka, a moderate who was nonetheless prepared to toe the Moscow line, had been put in office. To the outside world, the Soviets were clearly willing to go to great lengths to ensure the survival of the Warsaw Pact regardless of the opinions of outside powers.

Increasing tension

Indeed, despite his declared intention to create a more settled relationship with the West, Khrushchev was an unpredictable leader, given to public outbursts, and his time in office was full of crises which did nothing to ease the tensions between East and West. Once, at the United Nations, he took his shoe off and banged it on the table, shouting that the Soviet Union had its own nuclear missiles and no longer feared the possibility of an American attack.

To the Americans, the Soviet Union still seemed intent upon aggression, particularly when, in 1957, the communists appeared to gain a dangerous lead in nuclear capability. Before that date, there was no real danger of a Soviet nuclear strike on the United States, for the simple reason that the Soviets lacked the weapons with the necessary range. But in August 1957 Khrushchev announced that successful experiments had been carried out to test an intercontinental ballistic missile (ICBM), capable of travelling from the Soviet Union to American territory.

Less than two months later, the Soviets launched Sputnik I, the first-ever space satellite, and followed it up with Sputnik II, containing the dog Laika. Other than the fact that this was a major blow to American prestige, the implications seemed clear – if the Soviets could launch a satellite, their claims to have a viable ICBM could no longer be doubted. The Americans suddenly began to fear the potential consequences of the Cold War.

The missile gap

At first, the new developments appeared to boost the chances of a "thaw", or relaxation, in superpower relations, and in 1959 Khrushchev even visited the United States to pave the way for a summit meeting with Eisenhower in Paris the following spring. But the fear which fuelled the Cold War had been revived. Amid widespread calls in the United States (due to hold presidential elections in November 1960) for policies to close the supposed "missile gap" by a programme of ICBM development, the summit was doomed.

On 1 May 1960, as the two leaders were arriving in Paris, news came in that an American U-2 reconnaissance aircraft, flying high over the Soviet Union, had been shot down by a surface-to-air missile. Its pilot, Gary Powers, had been captured alive and the cameras, containing photographs of various military and industrial sites in the Soviet heartland, had survived. Khrushchev appeared at the summit demanding an instant apology from the Americans, punishment for those responsible and a promise that no more spying flights would take place. The flights were stopped – the development of satellites was making them no longer necessary – but Eisenhower refused to apologise. The Paris summit collapsed.

It was in this atmosphere of renewed tension that the Democrats won the 1960 presidential election and John Kennedy entered the White House. He had based his campaign on the need to close the missile gap, even though he was probably aware that such a gap did not in fact exist (even if it did, the Americans still enjoyed undoubted superiority of numbers and technology in nuclear terms), but his inauguration in January 1961 represented something much more profound. As the youngest-ever president, Kennedy seemed to encourage a feeling of hope in the future.

Unfortunately, such a hope was not immediately realised. Kennedy found it difficult to impose his personality on the American political establishment and this was reflected in his relations with the Soviets. Despite the failure of the Paris summit, another was scheduled to take place in Vienna in June 1961, and Kennedy did not succeed in impressing Khrushchev, who came away convinced that the new American president was weak. It was to take a series of fresh crises for this impression to be altered.

The Berlin Wall

The first of these crises had already begun to develop before Kennedy assumed the presidency. Khrushchev, eager to capitalise on Western desires to settle the future of Europe, had suggested a conference to negotiate a "deal" over the future of Germany, possibly along the same lines as that which had led to the Austrian State Treaty. The Western leaders had refused to compromise, however, and the split between the two Germanies remained.

This was also the case with Berlin, where the communists were experiencing a number of problems. Because the city was situated in the heart of East Germany, many people were taking the opportunity to "defect", simply by walking across the open border between the Soviet and Western sectors. By 1961, the problem was acute, for not only were huge numbers of people joining the exodus, but the vast majority were from the more professional classes of East German society, the loss of whom threatened the future of the country.

The division of Berlin: the Berlin Wall passes in front of the Brandenburg Gate (below), a symbol of Germany's glorious past. An East German escaper falls victim to guards in August 1962 (right).

Khrushchev responded by demanding that Berlin should be turned into a "free" city and that Western troops should be withdrawn. Kennedy refused. The more the Soviets increased the tension, the greater the exodus to the West by people fearful that it would soon be too late. During the last week of July 1961, 10,000 East Germans crossed the border.

Their fears were well justified. During the night of 12/13 August, East German soldiers closed the crossing points and began to construct a wall to block off the Soviet sector from the west. The wall provoked an immediate outcry from the Western powers: politicians denounced it and Kennedy sent his vice-president, Lyndon Johnson, to Berlin to assure the people of the Western sectors that they would not be deserted. The outcry reached new heights as people trying to escape across the wall into the West were shot down by East German border guards. The wall became, and still remains, a symbol of the East-West divide. To the West, it represents the denial of freedom in the East; to the East, it is essential to stop the movement of people westwards, and in their own words, to "prevent the insertion of Western agents and disruptive elements" into the Eastern bloc.

The Cuban Missile Crisis

But the most dangerous crisis between the superpowers, and one that came closest to open war, occurred over the island of Cuba. In January 1959 the revolutionary leader Fidel Castro led his followers into the capital, Havana, and overthrew the resident dictator, Fulgencio Batista. It was a triumph for the heady mixture of nationalism and left-wing (though not actually communist) ideologies that Castro had offered to the oppressed Cuban people, and there is little doubt that it took the United States by surprise. American companies lost valuable investments in the sugar and tobacco crops of Cuba.

The American government, fearing the spread of communism into their own "backyard" of Central and South America, reacted by imposing a strict economic blockade, hoping to starve Castro into submission to American policy. There is evidence that Castro was prepared to moderate his beliefs in the face of American pressure, but he could not cope with the blockade.

In desperation, he turned to the Soviets to redress the balance, a move that ensured his adherence to the ideals of communism which, in truth, he probably favoured. In February 1960, he signed a trade pact with the Soviet Union and in May the two countries established close diplomatic relations.

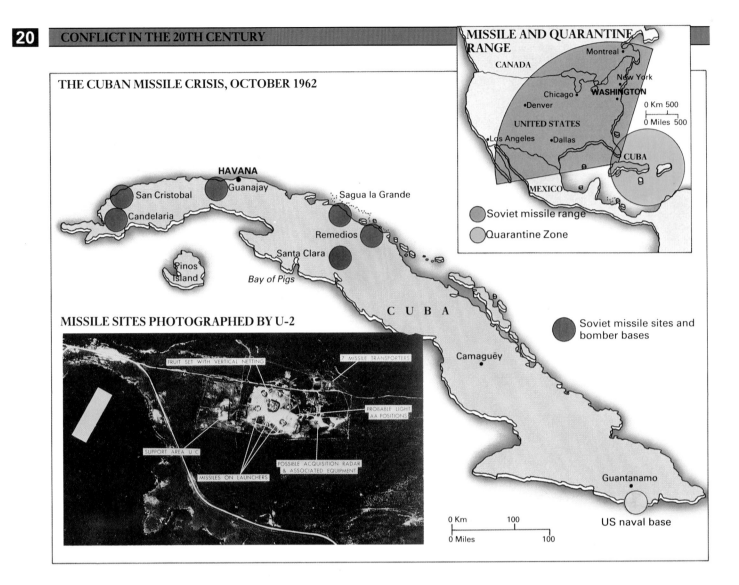

THE CUBAN MISSILE CRISIS, OCTOBER 1962

MISSILE AND QUARANTINE RANGE

CANADA

Montreal

New York

Chicago
WASHINGTON
Denver

UNITED STATES

Los Angeles · Dallas

0 Km 500
0 Miles 500

CUBA

MEXICO

Soviet missile range

Quarantine Zone

HAVANA

San Cristobal · Guanajay

Candelaria

Sagua la Grande

Remedios

Santa Clara

Pinos Island

Bay of Pigs

CUBA

Soviet missile sites and bomber bases

MISSILE SITES PHOTOGRAPHED BY U-2

FRUIT SET WITH VERTICAL NETTING

7 MISSILE TRANSPORTERS

PROBABLE LIGHT AA POSITIONS

SUPPORT AREA U C

MISSILES ON LAUNCHERS

POSSIBLE ACQUISITION RADAR & ASSOCIATED EQUIPMENT

Camagüey

Guantanamo

US naval base

0 Km 100
0 Miles 100

To the Americans, this was a highly dangerous development, threatening to introduce communism to a continent hitherto kept free of openly left-wing governments. Eisenhower authorised aid to Cuban exiles in the United States and the Central Intelligence Agency (CIA) began to train selected groups who were prepared to re-enter their homeland and overthrow Castro's government.

This was the plan inherited by Kennedy when he assumed the presidency in 1961. It was to end disastrously at the Bay of Pigs in April, with Castro proving well able to counter the poorly organised invasion. The boost to his prestige and the embarrassment to Kennedy were essential factors in what happened next.

By early 1962, Khrushchev was convinced that the Americans were weak. They had ceased to carry out U-2 reconnaissance missions over the Soviet Union after the capture of Gary Powers, Kennedy had seemed out of his depth at the Vienna summit and the Bay of Pigs invasion had suggested that the new president was afraid to confront Castro with his own forces. In such circumstances, the Soviets felt able to enter into a policy of "brinkmanship", seeing how far the Americans could be pushed before reacting. It was a dangerous strategy but one which, if it worked, could give the Soviet Union new advantages in the East-West balance. One of the most important of these advantages would be to gain some way of stationing nuclear missiles close to the United States, threatening such devastation that the Americans would be afraid to confront their enemy elsewhere.

Cuba was an obvious base for such missiles – the island is less than 144 km (90 miles) from the Florida coast – and from July 1962 the Americans began to receive disturbing reports of Soviet activities on the island. In August, a U-2 brought back pictures of new anti-aircraft facilities around Havana and in October Soviet aircraft capable of carrying nuclear weapons were spotted on the island. Then on 14 October came the most worrying evidence of all: another U-2 spotted what appeared to be launch sites for medium-range missiles which could reach most American cities. Two days later, Kennedy was informed by his intelligence chiefs that there was no doubt about Soviet intentions.

The president immediately convened a special "Executive Committee" of his closest advisers to monitor events and decide on policy moves. They considered an air strike against the missile sites and even the possibility of all-out invasion to topple Castro, but the chances of escalation to nuclear war were just too great.

Instead, in a televised speech to the American people on 22 October, Kennedy announced his intention to impose a naval blockade (he called it a "quarantine") around Cuba, through which no ships found to be carrying "offensive military equipment" would be allowed to pass. At the same time, American forces were to be placed on alert and Kennedy made it plain that any missile attack on the United States from the Cuban sites would be taken as a deliberate Soviet move and responded to accordingly.

The world waited with bated breath, aware that the slightest naval incident could trigger a nuclear war. On 25 October, the US Navy intercepted the first of 25 Soviet-chartered vessels known to be on their way to Cuba, but did not board her. Early the next morning the *Marucla*, known to be under charter to the Soviets, was stopped and searched. No offensive weapons were found and the *Marucla* was allowed to proceed, but the danger of conflict was acute. Fortunately, as 26 October progressed, reports began to come in that the other Soviet ships had halted, then that they had turned back. As Dean Rusk, a member of the Executive Committee, put it: "we're eyeball to eyeball and I think the other fellow just blinked".

Back from the brink
A message arrived from Khrushchev, stating that the Soviet Union was ready to relax the tension and would withdraw its missles from Cuba if the United States promised not to invade the island. Relief was short-lived, however, for within a matter of hours a second message insisted that the Americans also dismantle their missile sites in northern Turkey and withdraw nuclear weapons from both Britain and Italy, all of which were causing "uneasiness and anxiety" to the Soviets. Kennedy refused and the tempo of the crisis flared up again, particularly when a U-2 was shot down over Cuba and another, on a routine flight over Alaska, inadvertently strayed into Soviet airspace. War seemed inevitable.

Then the Americans had a brain-wave. They ignored Khrushchev's second letter and replied to the first, promising not to invade Cuba. It was just the sort of face-saving gesture that Khrushchev, by now aware that he had gone too far, desperately needed. Early on 28 October, at the end of 13 days of heart-stopping crisis, the Soviets agreed to withdraw their missiles from Cuba as soon as the United States agreed to demobilise the invasion forces gathered in Florida. Kennedy quickly responded and the level of tension declined, aided by unofficial indications to the Soviet ambassador in Washington that the American missiles in Turkey, already obsolete in an age of ICBMs, would be taken away.

The Cuban Missile Crisis was an undoubted triumph for Kennedy, showing that he was, after all, quite capable of coping with crises and of dealing with the pressures exerted by Khrushchev. Indeed, the humiliation suffered by the Soviet leader probably contributed to his downfall two years later, but this does not mean that the Soviets lost out entirely. The American pledge not to invade Cuba allowed them to turn what had been an insecure toehold in the Western Hemisphere into a firm foothold. Cuba became, and still is, an invaluable listening post from which the Soviet Union can monitor American naval movements in the Caribbean and, as future events were to show, a useful base from which to spread the ideals of communism into Central and South America, threatening the influence of the United States in an area of crucial strategic and economic importance.

When this coincided with a sudden growth of nationalism in certain Central and South American countries, based upon a reaction against existing right-wing, pro-United States governments, the problem was made even worse.

There was much more to the crisis than that, however, for it represented a turning-point in superpower relations during the post-1945 period. Up to October 1962, the various factors which created the Cold War – the different political beliefs, the clashes over territory in Europe and Korea, the fears prompted by the spread of nuclear weapons and the personality clashes between the various leaders of the superpowers – had seemed to push the world inevitably towards confrontation and war.

Cuba changed all that, reminding both sides that nuclear weapons introduced new pressures and responsibilities to the superpower divide, and although the basic causes of hostility did not disappear, a general desire to prevent similar crises began to take hold. The process was by no means immediate or easy, but a thaw in the Cold War was discernible. A new era of more responsible superpower relations was about to start.

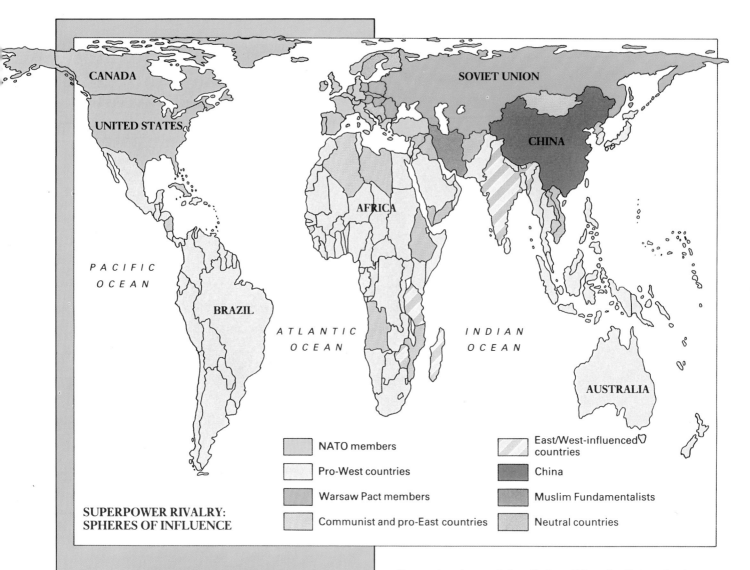

CANADA

UNITED STATES

SOVIET UNION

CHINA

AFRICA

PACIFIC OCEAN

BRAZIL

ATLANTIC OCEAN

INDIAN OCEAN

AUSTRALIA

NATO members	East/West-influenced countries
Pro-West countries	China
Warsaw Pact members	Muslim Fundamentalists
Communist and pro-East countries	Neutral countries

SUPERPOWER RIVALRY: SPHERES OF INFLUENCE

CHAPTER 2
DETENTE AND THE NEW COLD WAR

Since the Cuban Missile Crisis of October 1962, superpower relations have fluctuated. At first the superpowers followed the twin policies of "crisis management" and arms limitation. But although the traditional flashpoint of Europe became more settled, confrontation and hostility moved to the new arena of the Third World. By the early 1980s, amid signs that co-operation was a thing of the past, the superpowers drifted into a new Cold War.

Once the dust of the Cuban Missile Crisis had settled, both superpowers began to analyse recent events. There was no doubt that they had come dangerously close to war – Kennedy is on record as saying that he had "been to the edge of the abyss and looked over" – and their first reaction was to set up a means of preventing a repetition of such misunderstanding. On 20 June 1963, the "Hot-Line" Agreement was signed, creating a direct communication link between Washington and Moscow that would enable the two leaders to talk through their differences rather than merely react to events. It was the beginning of what was to become known as "detente".

Detente
Detente means, literally, the easing of tensions. The term comes from the days of the cross-bow and describes the action of releasing the taughtened string of the weapon without actually firing a bolt.

It aptly reflects superpower relations as they developed in the 1960s and early 1970s, for although neither side got rid of the awesome weapons at their disposal – indeed, the period was to see a massive increase in the capability of such weapons – they displayed a much more responsible attitude and an awareness of the consequences of hostility.

But if the initial motive for detente was fear, its roots went much deeper, reflecting changes to the superpower balance which would have had an effect even if the missile crisis had not occurred. By the early 1960s, it was obvious that the Soviet Union was catching up with the United States in nuclear capability, deploying ICBMs and the first of her submarine launched ballistic missiles (SLBMs), all able to hit the American homeland. The two superpowers probably achieved "nuclear parity", in which both had the ability to hit targets in the other's home territory, sometime in the mid-1960s. As parity was reached, the Americans, under the presidency of Lyndon Johnson after the

The "Hot-Line" nerve centre in Washington in 1974.

assassination of Kennedy in 1963, had no choice but to take a more careful line, searching for other alternatives to confrontation.

At the same time, Europe became more settled, lessening the chances of confrontation at the point where the two superpowers had their major forces. This reflected a growing belief that the territorial changes imposed in 1945 could not be altered by anything short of a suicidal war and, in the West at least, led to policies designed to make the best of the situation.

The European Community

In West Germany, for example, the ideal of reunification with the eastern part of the country was gradually dropped and relations with the other Western states improved. In September 1958, Konrad Adenauer of West Germany and Charles de Gaulle of France met in a spirit of friendship, having already agreed to co-operate in the creation of a European Economic Community (EEC), and in 1963 a Franco-German treaty was signed, burying the bitterness of two world wars.

Six years later, elections in West Germany led to victory for the Social Democrats and, under the chancellorship of Willy Brandt, the idea of improved relations was extended to the east. In August 1970, as part of a policy of *Ostpolitik* ("eastern politics"), Brandt negotiated a treaty with the Soviet Union which confirmed existing national frontiers, and this was followed by similar agreements with both Poland and East Germany.

In September 1971, the four occupying powers signed an agreement over Berlin – the Quadripartite Agreement – which settled some of the remaining differences in this traditional flashpoint city. Berlin was to stay totally separate from the two Germanies and the four powers were to maintain their troops in the various sectors. Channels for the settlement of disputes were carefully laid down.

By then, western Europe had become a much stronger region, chiefly through the EEC. Based on the Treaty of Rome, signed by Belgium, France, Italy, Luxembourg, the Netherlands and West Germany in March 1957, this was an attempt to create a "Common Market", free from trade barriers and economically strong, and there were hopes that this was merely a first step towards some form of close political union. As other countries joined – by 1986 Greece, Denmark, Ireland, Great Britain, Spain and Portugal had been added to the original six member states – it was obvious that western Europe was entering a more settled period.

The invasion of Czechoslovakia

At the same time, the Soviets were making sure that communist governments would continue to dominate eastern Europe within the borders of 1945. The process was by no means entirely peaceful, as events in Czechoslovakia in 1968 went to prove. At the beginning of that year Antonin Novotny, a hard-line communist, was replaced by the more liberal Alexander Dubček as leader of the country. Dubček and his followers, intent on introducing "socialism with a human face", set about loosening state control over the economy, abolishing censorship and opening up contacts with the West, while insisting that Czechoslovakia would remain a communist country and a member of the Warsaw Pact.

Pro-Dubček demonstrations in Prague (right), a week after the Soviet invasion (below), 1968.

They were heady days. During the "Prague Spring", the entire Czech nation seemed to come alive politically. With free speech allowed for the first time, the streets of the capital, Prague, were filled with people taking part in political discussions, holding impromptu meetings and distributing uncensored literature. Hardly surprisingly, the Soviets became alarmed, seeing the dangers to their control over eastern Europe if such liberal views spread elsewhere in the Warsaw Pact.

At first, they attempted negotiation, meeting the new Czech leaders on a train on the Soviet-Czech border, but when this did not produce results, they resolved to use force instead. In August 1968, under the guise of Warsaw Pact manoeuvres, an invasion force was put together and the tanks sent in. The Czechs were caught by surprise, offering little more resistance than demonstrations on the streets of Prague. Dubček was forced to stand down, to be replaced by a pro-Moscow communist leader, Gustav Husak, and the reforms of 1968 were overthrown.

The Soviets succeeded in this policy for two main reasons. First, they chose the moment for invasion carefully, lulling the Czechs into a false sense of security and waiting until Western attention was elsewhere – in this case Vietnam, where the Americans were bogged down in an unpopular war, and Paris, where student unrest (widespread throughout the liberal democracies in 1968) had threatened to burst into full-scale revolution.

Second, the Soviets were aware that the relatively settled state of Europe made it unlikely that the West would respond to the Czechoslovak troubles with anything more than verbal or diplomatic complaints. The borders of Europe, and with them the reality of Soviet control of the eastern bloc, had become an accepted state of affairs. Just to reinforce the point, Leonid Brezhnev, the man who had gained power in Moscow in the aftermath of Khrushchev's downfall in the mid-1960s, declared his right to intervene in the affairs of countries within the Soviet "sphere of influence" – a declaration that was to become known as the "Brezhnev Doctrine".

The policies of detente

Thus, detente developed in an atmosphere of enforced calm based upon nuclear equality and European settlement rather than one of new understanding or friendship. This was reflected in the sorts of policies adopted by the two sides. The superpowers did not trust each other, they had merely learned to live with each other. The motives for detente differed in both Washington and Moscow. To the Americans, detente was a means of controlling Soviet actions, preventing the sort of aggressive foreign policy and brinkmanship that had culminated in Cuba in October 1962.

This was to be achieved in a number of ways. On the economic front, the Americans recognised that the Soviets were desperate for high technology and grain, both of which could be provided by the West. If the Soviets therefore became dependent upon the West, supplies of such essential commodities could be made conditional on the "good behaviour" of the Soviets, who would be so entangled in a "web" of economic agreements that they would be unable to take an independent line.

Similarly, if the Americans could play the "China card" by improving relations between Washington and Peking, the Soviets would become alarmed and would cease to create crises for fear of a war on two fronts. This was made possible by the political and ideological split that had emerged between the two communist powers in the 1960s, culminating in border clashes on the Ussuri River in 1969. After this, the Soviet Union was threatened by attack from the south as well as the west so far as the politburo was concerned. Richard Nixon, who replaced Johnson as US president in 1968, was particularly adept at this policy of playing off one communist superpower against the other, visiting China in February 1972.

Unfortunately, Soviet definitions of detente were different. As they were never going to allow themselves to be controlled by the West, they preferred to use the new atmosphere of superpower relations to divert Western attention away from their more global policies. For some time, the politburo had been convinced that the series of crises between East and West – Berlin in 1948-49, Hungary in 1956, Berlin in 1961, Cuba in 1962 – had helped to strengthen the resolve of Western powers, giving them something concrete to fear and forcing them to react to the spread of Soviet influence wherever it might appear.

If the West could be lulled into a sense of trust and security, the Soviets would be free to pursue their policy objectives in the Third World – the key regions of the globe that were neither industrialised liberal democracies (First World) nor established communist states (Second World). In addition, Brezhnev was keen to get access to Western technology to modernise Soviet industry and was aware that this would not be possible in an atmosphere of hostility.

An uneasy calm
These differences of definition were to undermine the process of detente by the mid-1970s, but it would be wrong to presume that nothing was achieved. Regardless of underlying motives, both superpowers were interested in pursuing policies of co-operation in two important areas. The first of these was "crisis management", for both sides recognised that if ideological or territorial clashes were allowed to develop unchecked, the chances of nuclear war were very high indeed. The signing of the Hot-Line Agreement in 1963 was an essential first step in this direction, giving the two sides an ability to put forward their respective views clearly and precisely, so that misunderstandings could be kept to a minimum.

Superpower "spheres of influence" were respected – for example, the Americans made no moves actively to prevent the Soviet invasion of Czechoslovakia in 1968 and, for a time, the Soviets did little to support Cuban policies towards Latin America. When crises did occur, genuine attempts were made to prevent unnecessary escalation. In June 1967, during the Six-Day War between Israel and her Arab neighbours, for example, the Americans moved elements of their Sixth Fleet close to the Israeli coast, carefully explaining to the Soviets that this was in response to Israeli attacks on the American ship USS *Liberty* and not a deliberately provocative gesture against the Soviets' Arab allies.

The second area of "common ground" concerned nuclear weapons, for by the late 1960s both sides were aware of the need for a balance of capability in which neither superpower would enjoy sufficient advantage to gain a "victory" and so be tempted to launch a surprise attack. There were a number of ways in which such an advantage might be gained. Both sides had the ability to station weapons in suitable areas for a surprise attack – notably outer space and the seabed. Also both were actively pursuing the idea of anti-ballistic missiles (ABMs) which could be used to destroy enemy nuclear warheads before they hit their targets.

At the same time, the spread of nuclear weapons to other countries (a process known as "proliferation") needed checking in case an ambitious or irresponsible government developed its own nuclear weapons. Also something had to be done to control the testing of nuclear warheads in case of damage to the world's environment. Finally, both sides were attracted by the prospect of "arms control", mutual agreements to limit the development or deployment of weapons systems, for this would save money.

A number of agreements emerged. As early as 25 July 1963, a Nuclear Test-Ban Treaty was signed, prohibiting nuclear testing in the atmosphere, and this was followed on 27 February 1967 by an Outer Space Treaty which banned the deployment of weapons of mass destruction in orbit around the Earth. On 1 July 1968, the countries of the United Nations were invited to sign the Non-Proliferation Treaty, promising to refrain from acquiring nuclear weapons. Although this was seriously undermined when a number of countries on the threshold of nuclear capability – including Argentina, Brazil, India, Israel, Pakistan and South Africa – refused to sign, the fact that 124 states did was a significant development. Of equal importance was the Seabed Treaty, signed by the superpowers on 11 February 1971, for this prevented them from placing nuclear mines at key "chokepoints" in the world's oceans, ready to explode should a war begin.

The SALT talks
These negotiations were not particularly difficult in that they did not immediately affect the security of the superpower homelands. The same was not the case when the superpowers turned to arms control, for although the Strategic Arms Limitation Talks (SALT) began in Helsinki in November 1969, it was to take nearly three years for an agreement to be reached. The problems were immense. Both sides were interested in limiting the development of ABMs because of the crippling expense that would be involved, and both were aware that the nuclear balance was under threat. However, they found it extremely difficult to agree to a common "ceiling" of weapons numbers beyond which they would not go.

One of the main difficulties was the matter of defining just what should be included in the talks. The weapons under discussion were meant to be "strategic". However, to the Americans, this covered those nuclear weapons which, when fired from one superpower homeland, had the range to reach the other; to the Soviets, it included all weapons which might be fired at the Soviet Union, regardless of range – a definition that included those missiles and aircraft of the Western alliance that were stationed in Europe. The situation was not helped by the fact that the nuclear arsenals of the superpowers were not evenly matched: the Soviets had concentrated on large, heavy land-based missiles while the Americans had begun to deploy lighter, more accurate weapons, fitted with more than one warhead.

Brezhnev addresses the CSCE in Helsinki, 1975.

The result was a lengthy process of negotiation, but some success was achieved. At a summit meeting in Moscow in May 1972, Nixon and Brezhnev signed two linked agreements known as SALT I. The first, an Interim Agreement on Strategic Offensive Arms, froze the number of strategic nuclear launchers (missiles, bombers and submarines) permitted to each side, and although the Soviets refused to say precisely how many they had, the figures were generally reckoned to be 1,054 on the American side and 1,618 on the Soviet. The agreement was to last for five years only and was to be treated as the first step to more detailed negotiations designed to set a common ceiling.

The second agreement, the Anti-Ballistic Missile Treaty, was of indefinite duration. Each superpower was to be allowed two ABM systems only, one around its capital city and the other around an ICBM launch-site, the idea being that in neither case would complete defence be assured – there would always be large parts of the population unprotected, acting as hostages to nuclear strikes which neither side would actually dare to initiate.

SALT did not end there, for the creation of a common ceiling was essential if the arms race was to be controlled. In July 1974, Nixon travelled again to Moscow to sign a Threshold Test-Ban Treaty, limiting the size of nuclear weapons tests. Five months later, Nixon's successor, President Gerald Ford, met Brezhnev at Vladivostok in eastern Russia to finalise ceiling figures. Both sides agreed to limit their numbers to 2,400 strategic weapons platforms, of which 1,320 could contain multiple re-entry vehicles (MRVs) – weapons with the capability of carrying more than one warhead – and arrangements were made for negotiations designed to bring that ceiling down.

The Helsinki Accords

SALT was a major breakthrough and one that acted as a spur to other negotiations between the superpower blocs. On 30 October 1973, the Mutual and Balanced Force Reduction (MBFR) talks began in Vienna between NATO and Warsaw Pact countries, aiming to reduce the number of troops and weapons stationed in central Europe, and two years later all the countries of Europe (except Albania) met in Helsinki for a Conference on Security and Co-operation in Europe (CSCE).

The latter led to an agreement, usually known as the Helsinki Accords, signed on 1 August 1975, which is often seen as the high point of detente. Together with the United States and Canada, the Europeans on both sides of the political divide accepted the frontiers drawn up in 1945, effectively recognising the reality of the Soviet-created buffer zone of eastern Europe. In return for this formal "blessing" by the West – something that the Soviets had been seeking since the end of the Second World War – the Soviet Union and her allies promised to respect and improve the human rights of their citizens. These rights included more freedom for eastern bloc citizens to disagree with their governments in speech and writing, freedom to hold meetings, to travel and to join members of their families living in the West.

The human rights pledges were to prove embarrassing to the Soviet Union, particularly at the regular follow-up conferences that subsequently took place, for the West lost no opportunity to highlight abuses. However, the mere fact that an agreement had been signed seemed to imply a new spirit of freedom. The Helsinki Accords also dealt with East-West trade and further contributed to the stability of Europe through agreed "Confidence Building Measures" (CBMs) to reduce misunderstandings over military movements. Henceforth, all countries agreed to give notice in advance about military manoeuvres or exercises involving more than 25,000 troops, to remove fears of surprise attack.

SALT II

While the CSCE details were being discussed and carried out, the superpowers continued their negotiations about nuclear weapons, aiming to produce SALT II. The process was not easy, for whereas SALT I had dealt with numbers of delivery vehicles – things that could be seen and counted – technology had begun to complicate matters to a significant extent. As both sides deployed missiles with multiple warheads, it was no longer possible to tell at a glance what was available, for a single missile might contain up to 10 multiple re-entry vehicles, each capable of hitting an individual target with impressive accuracy.

In addition, in the years immediately after the Vladivostok meeting, both sides introduced new weapons which were difficult to assess. On the American side, for example, the cruise missile – a highly accurate and extremely small delivery vehicle, capable of deployment from both aircraft and submarines in the 1970s – did not seem to fit the definitions of "strategic" hammered out in SALT I. The same applied on the Soviet side to the Tupolev Tu-26 "Backfire" bomber. In the latter case, the Americans wanted the weapon included in the strategic total, arguing that with in-flight refuelling it could reach the United States with nuclear bombs on board, whereas the Soviets pointed out that by this definition, almost any aircraft had strategic capability.

The Soviet Tu-26 "Backfire" bomber.

Because of such arguments, the negotiations stalled and it was not until May 1979, by which time Ford had been replaced as US president by Jimmy Carter, that SALT II was signed in Vienna. The force ceilings laid down at Vladivostok were confirmed and an agreement made that these would be gradually reduced until both sides had no more than 2,250 weapons, of which 1,200 could contain multiple independently targeted re-entry vehicles (MIRVs).

The Boeing AGM-86B ALCM (air-launched cruise missile) during a test flight.

The problem of the Backfire bomber was dealt with by a Soviet statement that the aircraft was of medium-range and that there was no intention of giving it inter-continental range. Similarly, in a Protocol which was to remain in force until 31 December 1981, cruise missiles with ranges of more than 600km (375 miles) were banned. The main treaty was to last until 1985, by which time, it was hoped, negotiations for SALT III would have been carried out.

SALT II was unsatisfactory on a number of counts. In real terms, it achieved no significant reduction in nuclear forces, and provided only half-hearted attempts to resolve the issues raised by new weapons. To many people, particularly in the United States, the treaty seemed to allow the Soviets to match American capability, undermining the West's technological advantage. When Carter presented the details to the US Senate for ratification, it looked as if the agreement would be rejected. Detente had suddenly gone sour.

The Vietnam War

This was hardly surprising. By 1979 there were already clear signs that the hopes of detente had not been realised. America's aim of controlling Soviet actions through economic dependence and the "China card" had failed to prevent a series of crises in the Third World, most of which seemed to confirm a substantial decline in the prestige of the United States. This had its origins in the Vietnam War. Although no one doubted the military power of the United States when she first committed troops to the defence of South Vietnam in 1965, that power had failed to prevent a humiliating US withdrawal in 1973 and a communist takeover of the South two years later.

The impact of these events was enormous. On the military side, they suggested that the Americans were afraid to use the full potential of their forces to achieve victory. They preferred to fight a "limited war" in which political leaders in Washington kept a close and inhibiting hold over the armed forces, restricting the number of men available in Vietnam, the weapons in use and the targets to be hit. There was no attempt, for example, to invade North Vietnam and, with the exception of a short period in 1972, no deliberate bombing of enemy civilian centres in Hanoi or Haiphong.

In a strategic sense, this was understandable – the Americans had no wish to draw the Soviets into the war (something that could have happened if they felt that their allies in North Vietnam were about to be destroyed) and were quite content to fight just to preserve

the status quo – but it did nothing to boost the confidence of the US armed forces. By the early 1970s, American morale in the war zone was declining, and by 1973 the combat effectiveness of the army was seriously in question.

But it was the political results of Vietnam that were important. As US casualties mounted, opposition to the war grew in the United States itself and people lost confidence in their leaders. For example, President Johnson decided not to stand for re-election in 1968 largely because his promises of victory in Vietnam had been seen to be false during the Tet Offensive, when North Vietnamese and Viet Cong forces attacked towns and cities throughout the South.

Although Nixon was elected specifically to "bring the boys home" from an unpopular war, he was forced to continue the fighting until 1973. His subsequent involvement in the Watergate scandal, when it was discovered that he had known about (if not personally authorised) attempts to spy on his political opponents in the United States, further contributed to a decline of confidence. The communist victory in Vietnam, followed closely by similar successes in Laos and Cambodia, seemed merely to confirm that the Americans were neither willing nor able to support their allies in the Third World.

America in retreat

The result was a period of American "soul searching" which lasted from about 1975 until the election of Ronald Reagan as president in 1980. It was a period characterised by a lack of resolve in foreign policy as domestic affairs took precedence. If detente had achieved the sort of international control it had aimed at, this would not have mattered, but the Soviets, convinced that the Americans were weak, took every opportunity to exploit the situation.

To them, detente was something that only affected superpower relations. Although improved security in Europe was undoubtedly a major achievement, the Soviets saw no reason to presume that detente should alter their policies towards the Third World, particularly when those policies stood a good chance of succeeding in the absence of American opposition.

As the 1970s progressed, therefore, the Soviets began to interfere in a number of key areas. They used the continuance of detente to lull the Americans into a false sense of security and ruthlessly exploited every sign of weakness to gain advantage and extend their sphere of influence.

In 1976, the Soviets used Cuban troops to ensure the success of communist forces in the Angolan civil war, fending off attacks from Zairean and South African columns which had expected American backing, and a year later Soviet supplies and yet more Cuban soldiers ensured the survival of the pro-communist regime in Ethiopia when it was attacked from neighbouring Somalia. In both cases, the outcome was a communist presence in countries of strategic importance – Angola lies perilously close to the mineral resources of South Africa, on which the West depends, while Ethiopia controls access to the trading routes of the Red Sea. Yet the Americans made no counter-moves.

Above: A Cuban adviser in Angola, 1976.
Below: Ayatollah Khomeini in Iran, 1979.

American weakness reached a critical point over Iran in 1979-80. The United States did nothing to protect the Shah of Iran, one of the most important pro-Western leaders in the Middle East, when he was opposed by Muslim fundamentalists under the Ayatollah Khomeini. America then faced the humiliation of seeing their Embassy in Tehran stormed and more than 50 diplomats held hostage. Their captors demanded that America send the Shah back to Iran – he had fled the country in January 1979 – and for over a year, from the seizure of the Embassy in November 1979 to the release of the hostages in exchange for American concessions in January 1981, the American people were forced to accept that, regardless of its awesome power, their country could do little to prevent such incidents.

The mounting tide of frustration, fuelled by the failure of a helicopter rescue mission in April 1980 (Operation Eagle Claw) in which eight American servicemen lost their lives, undoubtedly helped to ensure the election of Reagan to the White House in November 1980. His strident calls for policies to increase the effective power of the United States – to make the country "walk tall" on the world stage – did nothing to ease the strains between the superpowers.

Afghanistan and the end of detente

But this was hardly the fault of Reagan, for by 1980 the West as a whole was convinced that the Soviets were abusing detente to gain new strategic advantages. The turning-point was Afghanistan, invaded by Soviet forces in late December 1979. This was the first time since 1945 that the Soviet leadership had felt confident enough to send its troops outside the Warsaw Pact area, extending its influence through force of arms.

On Christmas night 1979, a force of between 4,000 and 5,000 Soviet troops – men of the crack 105th Guards Airborne Division – were airlifted into the Afghan capital, Kabul, where they led an assault on the presidential palace, killing the president and replacing him with the Soviets' protege, Babrak Karmal. Within hours, an estimated 50,000 motorised rifle troops and 1,000 tanks had crossed the border from the Soviet Union, seizing the major towns and communications routes. By January 1980, the invasion force numbered over 85,000 men.

The international outcry was immediate – on 14 January the United Nations General Assembly roundly condemned such a blatant use of force – and superpower relations declined to a point untouched since the Cold War of the early 1960s. President Carter, with an eye to elections later in the year, placed an immediate freeze on the sale of grain to the Soviet Union, suspended the export of high technology and began organising a Western boycott of the Olympic Games, due to be held in Moscow in the summer.

According to the original theory of detente in the United States, Soviet dependence upon such commodities as grain and technology should have deterred them from continued military action in Afghanistan, but this did not happen. The Soviets effectively ignored the American response, preferring to suffer the loss of imports rather than halt an invasion that the politburo deemed essential to the security of the state.

They were determined to restore a "friendly" regime in the Afghan capital, particularly because of the sudden growth of Muslim fundamentalism in Iran, further to the west. If this should spread into Afghanistan, it might go on to affect the substantial Muslim population of the southern republics of the Soviet Union and so weaken the hold of communism in an important area. In addition, a Soviet presence in Afghanistan would put them in an ideal position from which to exploit the weaknesses of Iran, satisfying a long-held ambition to gain a port in the Arabian (Persian) Gulf.

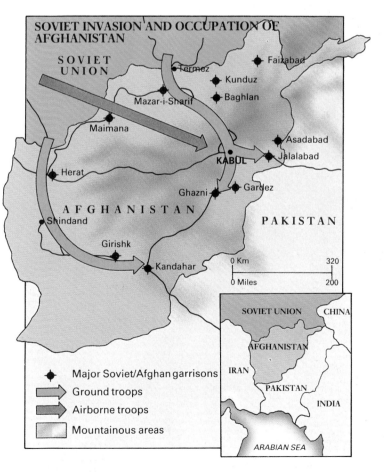

The Soviets' Vietnam

Unfortunately for the Soviets, the invasion soon proved to be the beginning of a nightmare, for instead of swiftly asserting communist power it degenerated into a costly, drawn-out war against anti-communist Muslim rebels known as *mujaheddin* ("holy warriors"). Like the Americans in Vietnam, the Soviet superpower found itself involved in extremely inhospitable terrain, fighting guerrillas whose intimate knowledge of the mountains and widespread support among the ordinary people gave them significant advantages.

The Soviet invasion force, organised as if for a major war in Europe, soon found that its heavy tanks and mechanised infantry were useless against the hit-and-run tactics of the *mujaheddin*, and worrying reports of demoralisation among the soldiers began to appear. The situation was not helped by the virtual disintegration of the Afghan Army, many of whose members were quick to desert as soon as fighting began.

The Soviets were forced to alter their tactics to cope with this unexpected war. Tank units were withdrawn, to be replaced by more mobile armoured combat vehicles, convoys of trucks travelling along vulnerable roads were protected and airpower was used to hit the guerrillas' mountain bases. By the mid-1980s, the Soviets were still bogged down in Afghanistan and the *mujaheddin* threat was still strong, although the use of helicopter gunships, concentrated "sweep and destroy" advances into guerrilla-held territory and even a reported use of chemical weapons had prevented a Soviet defeat. Even so, their forces continued to control little beyond the major towns and the drain on the economy and manpower of the Soviet Union was apparent.

Worsening relations

International condemnation of Soviet actions had not died down. A number of countries, including Egypt, Saudi Arabia and China, showed their displeasure by giving military and economic aid to the *mujaheddin*, but it was in the United States that Afghanistan had its most lasting effect. The Soviet invasion certainly persuaded Carter that detente was no longer of any value.

War in Afghanistan: mujaheddin *with a heavy machine gun in the Panjsher Valley prepare for action.*

Indeed, in addition to the trade sanctions, the United States refused to ratify (finally accept) SALT II. During the last months of his presidency a distinct chill fell over the superpower relationship. Old fears of communist expansion were revived and moves made towards renewed containment.

Carter declared that the Persian Gulf was an area central to American strategic interests, establishing a permanent US naval presence in the region and creating a special "Rapid Deployment Joint Task Force" (RDJTF) of airmobile troops ready to be sent to the Gulf in the event of a crisis. Negotiations began with Egypt, Morocco, Oman, Kenya and Somalia to provide military bases for the RDJTF, Britain was persuaded to lease the island of Diego Garcia in the Indian Ocean and military exercises were planned.

A new arms build-up

Once distrust between the superpowers had re-emerged in this way, it was quickly extended to other areas, not least Europe, where a Soviet build-up of arms had been noted. By the late 1970s, a new generation of medium-range nuclear missiles had appeared in the Soviet Union – mobile SS-20s, capable of hitting targets in western Europe but not powerful enough to reach the United States.

In November 1979 NATO responded by announcing the deployment of its own improved medium-range "theatre" weapons. A total of 464 ground-launched cruise missiles (GLCMs) and 108 Pershing II rockets were to be stationed, under American control, in Britain, West Germany, Belgium, Italy and the Netherlands unless the Soviets agreed to negotiate a new arms control agreement that would lead to a removal of the SS-20s. The first GLCMs arrived at Greenham Common airbase in England in November 1983. No new arms agreement had been made and the SS-20s were still firmly in place.

Poland

The Soviets seemed to be adopting hard-line policies, and this view was reinforced in the eyes of the West by events in Poland. In August 1980, a wave of unrest began in the country, led by shipyard workers at the port of Gdansk. Most of the confrontations with the communist government concerned Solidarity, a newly-formed independent trade union which quickly attracted over eight million members. The Polish government proved weak in the face of such opposition and, after negotiations with Solidarity's leader, Lech

Walesa, the Gdansk Agreement was signed, giving the workers the right to strike and promising less censorship, shorter working hours and higher wages.

The Soviets, ever fearful of the spread of "liberal" ideas in the eastern bloc, viewed the crisis with growing concern, and although they did not repeat the pattern of armed intervention established in Hungary in 1956 and Czechoslovakia in 1968, they did all they could behind the scenes to bolster up the Polish government, led by General Wojciech Jaruzelski. As trouble flared up throughout the country and Solidarity demanded free elections to the Polish parliament, Soviet leaders began to mass troops on the border, convinced that the Polish government was about to be overthrown.

On 13 December 1981 Jaruzelski responded by imposing martial law and banning all trade union activity. As Solidarity members were arrested, the West protested, blaming the Soviets. The Americans stopped the supply of food to Poland and the Soviet Union and tried to extend this to include overall trade sanctions. By then, however, the European allies had moderated their stance, particularly when Soviet forces on the Polish border dispersed, and Poland was left to sort out its own problems. Martial law was officially lifted in July 1983, although laws extending the control of the government remained in force.

The New Cold War

The fact that the Polish crisis did not produce a full-scale superpower confrontation implied that there was still a residue of detente in the air, but this was a false hope. Many of the characteristics of the Cold War had re-emerged – fear of nuclear war, territorial rivalry and basic mistrust – and when these were reinforced by the rhetoric of Reagan, determined to portray the United States as a champion of liberal democracy and freedom and the Soviet Union as an "evil empire", it was not long before people were sensing a new atmosphere of superpower tension, dubbing it the "New Cold War".

So far as the Americans were concerned, the Soviets had become dangerously powerful and intent upon extending their influence, and nowhere was this more true than in the United States' own "backyard", Central America. This was an area that the Americans could not ignore, particularly as it contained the Panama Canal, crucial to the movement of naval and merchant shipping between the Pacific and Atlantic Oceans, and they had done much in the past to ensure that communism did not spread there from Cuba or the Soviet Union.

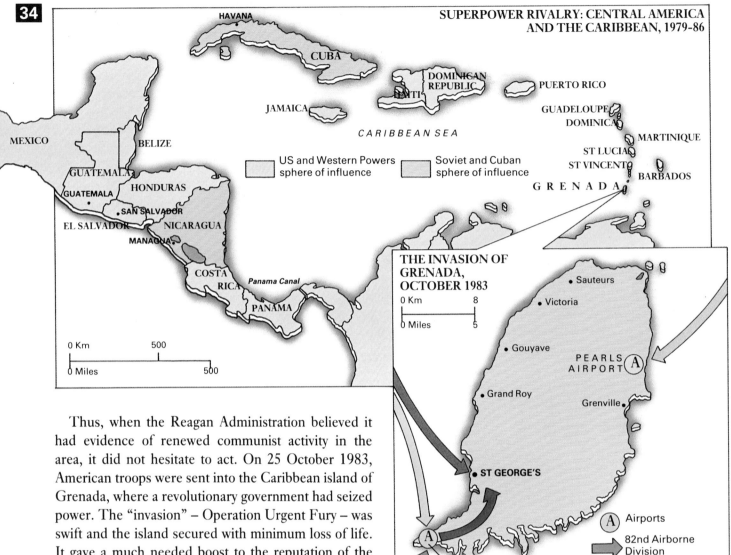

US and Western Powers sphere of influence

Soviet and Cuban sphere of influence

THE INVASION OF GRENADA, OCTOBER 1983

0 Km — 8
0 Miles — 5

(A) Airports

82nd Airborne Division

Task Force air raids, helicopter troops

Marines' and Rangers' attack

22nd Marine Amphibious Unit

Airborne Rangers Units

POINT SALINES

Thus, when the Reagan Administration believed it had evidence of renewed communist activity in the area, it did not hesitate to act. On 25 October 1983, American troops were sent into the Caribbean island of Grenada, where a revolutionary government had seized power. The "invasion" – Operation Urgent Fury – was swift and the island secured with minimum loss of life. It gave a much needed boost to the reputation of the American armed forces, still trying to live down the humiliation of Vietnam.

Reagan openly accused the Soviets of interfering in the affairs of Central America and the Caribbean, but he proved wary of committing his own forces to more difficult operations. In Nicaragua, where the left wing Sandinistas had overthrown the corrupt dictatorship of General Anastasio Somoza in 1979, the Americans preferred to offer aid to anti-government forces – the "Contras" – accusing the Sandinistas of spreading communism into neighbouring countries.

Chief among these was El Salvador, where a military-civilian junta was being opposed by Marxist-Leninist guerrilla groups, and Reagan authorised military and economic aid, in this case to bolster up the existing regime. In both countries – Nicaragua and El Salvador – there was certainly evidence of Cuban involvement among the anti-American groups, but in all cases the Americans ignored the popular appeal of nationalism. To many Americans Reagan's response was understandable, even if it did little to ease the East-West tensions.

Nuclear balances

At the same time, both superpowers continued to increase and improve their nuclear stockpiles – the Americans introduced a new class of nuclear-armed submarine, the "Ohio", and a new ICBM, the MX "Peacekeeper", in the early 1980s, while the Soviets deployed the "Blackjack" bomber and experimented with a new generation of ICBMs – and proved unwilling seriously to discuss the next round of arms limitation.

In November 1981, the Intermediate-Range Nuclear Force (INF) talks began in Geneva, covering the question of the SS-20s and GLCMs in Europe, and in June 1982, the two superpowers met in the same Swiss city for the opening round of the Strategic Arms Reduction Talks (START). During this period there was growing public disquiet in western Europe about nuclear weapons, voiced by a variety of disarmament and peace groups which have enjoyed increasing popular support in recent years. However, neither set of negotiations produced an agreement. By the end of 1983 the talks had effectively ceased.

They had not been helped by Reagan's announcement on 23 March 1983 that the United States would pursue research into a space-based anti-missile defence system, officially known as the Strategic Defense Initiative (SDI) but popularly called "Star Wars". It seemed to be a direct threat to the careful balance of capabilities, promising the Americans a degree of protection the Soviets could not match. Although SDI was extremely futuristic – it is unlikely to be deployed before the turn of the century, presuming that technology can produce the weapons in that time – it drove the wedge yet deeper between the superpowers.

But it would be wrong to presume that the New Cold War left the world on the brink of destruction. Despite the higher incidence of crises since the mid-1970s, none had even approached the danger of the Cuban Missile Crisis of 1962, and despite the failure of arms control in recent years, both sides were still willing to talk. In the immediate aftermath of the SDI announcement, the Soviets indicated a willingness to resume "talks about talks" in Geneva, and these proved to be a useful way of getting the superpowers together.

The process was helped by the sudden change of leadership in the Soviet Union. Brezhnev died in November 1982, to be followed in quick succession by Yuri Andropov and Konstantin Chernenko, and finally in March 1985 by the relatively young Mikhail Gorbachev, aged 54. He announced a number of arms control proposals, including a moratorium on Soviet nuclear tests, and in November 1985 he and Reagan met for a summit in Geneva. This produced little by way of concrete results, stalling over American unwillingness to stop research into SDI, but for a time the tension seemed to be reduced.

How far this acted as a basis for improved relations depended upon future events, although in an atmosphere of mutual distrust, the signs were not good. To the Americans, Soviet policies towards Afghanistan, Central America and parts of Africa constituted a major threat to world peace and had to be opposed; to the Soviets, America's new-found confidence, improved armed forces and willingness to spend on SDI indicated a level of power which could not be matched, thereby undermining the security of the Soviet Union. So long as such distrust remained, a settled superpower relationship was impossible: the Cold War was likely to continue.

As US cruise missiles arrive at Greenham Common in England, women "peace protesters" continue their vigil.

CHAPTER 3
THE NUCLEAR BACKCLOTH

Since 1945, the world has faced the possibility of nuclear war. The destruction of the Japanese cities of Hiroshima and Nagasaki acts as a constant reminder of the awesome power of even the smallest nuclear weapon, and this has been reinforced by the knowledge that technology constantly increases the size and potential of nuclear forces. By the mid-1980s, the five countries known to possess nuclear weapons could have destroyed the world four times over. As the main nuclear stockpiles are held by the two rival superpowers – the United States and Soviet Union – the chances of a war involving such weapons are always strong. Peace has been maintained through "deterrence", in which neither side dares to attack the other for fear of the consequences, but this is by no means secure. The Cold War world exists on a knife-edge of uncertainty.

By July 1945, researchers at the American Manhattan Project had perfected a "fission" device, creating an atomic chain reaction by firing two pieces of Uranium 235 into each other by means of small conventional explosions. After an initial test at Alamogordo, in the New Mexico desert, bombs were made ready for use against Japan. The results were terrifying: at 8.15 am on 6 August 1945, 80,000 people died in Hiroshima. Three days later, 39,000 were killed in Nagasaki.

By today's standards, these bombs were relatively small – both produced explosions equivalent to 20,000 tons of TNT – but it did not take long to develop the next generation, of seemingly limitless power. These were "fusion" weapons, based upon the idea that if the hydrogen nuclei of deuterium and tritium are compressed together with sufficient force, they will be fused to create helium and release enormous bursts of energy. The Americans test-fired such a "hydrogen" or "thermonuclear" bomb in November 1952 and the Soviets developed one soon after. Since that time most weapons have been based upon this process. The "yield", or explosive power, of such weapons can equal millions of tonnes equivalent in TNT (megatons); in 1963 the Soviets tested a device estimated at 58 megatons, more than enough to destroy a small country virtually on its own.

If nuclear weapons were ever used, the effects would be appalling. A one-megaton warhead, for example, would produce a searing flash of light which would blind anyone looking towards it up to 160 km (100 miles) away, while the heat generated by the explosion would rival that of the sun, melting anything within 5 km (3 miles) of the point of impact and burning people standing as far away as 32 km (20 miles).

Buildings would disappear under the force of a huge blast wave and radioactive dust, falling to earth for weeks afterwards, would spread sickness and lingering death. Finally, the electromagnetic pulse produced by the explosion would cut out all telephones, radios and computers over a wide area. A study by the US Congress in 1980 estimated that such an explosion 1,800 m (6,000 ft) in the air over the city of Detroit would kill 470,000 people and injure 630,000. By the time this study was made, the two superpowers between them had more than 17,000 warheads capable of delivering such a weapon.

Left: Hiroshima, photographed in March 1946.
Below: Polaris missile tubes on the USS Sam Rayburn.

Deterrence

The development of such instantaneous destructive capability has had a profound effect upon the use of force in international politics. Before nuclear weapons, any country feeling threatened could start a war without risking complete and guaranteed devastation. This is no longer the case, at least for the five nuclear powers of the present age – the United States, Soviet Union, Britain, China and France.

They may still be able to use their conventional (non-nuclear) forces against less powerful countries which do not possess nuclear weapons, but if they confront each other, the danger is enormous. In such circumstances, relations between nuclear-capable countries cannot be based on a policy of military superiority, in which forces are used to fight and win wars; they must be based instead upon war-prevention. Since the 1940s, this has been achieved through "deterrence".

All of us experience the principle of deterrence in our ordinary, everyday lives. As children, we are deterred from doing things our parents or teachers do not want us to do by threats of punishment.

Nuclear deterrence is no different: what one superpower is saying to the other is that if certain policies are pursued nuclear weapons, with their proven destructive power, are available to counter them. Thus, the potential enemy must think twice about the merits of such policies, and make a "cost-gain" calculation – "is what I am after worth the risk of nuclear devastation?" If he is rational, he should be put off or deterred. In more official language, deterrence is "the ability to prevent aggression by persuading a potential enemy that the gains to be had by undertaking a particular course of action are outweighed by the losses he will suffer if he persists"; in other words, "if you hit me I can and will hit you back harder".

For this to work, certain conditions must be met. It is no good, for example, trying to deter someone who does not believe that you will ever carry out your threat or if you quite clearly lack the means to do so – factors which usually go under the titles of "credibility" and "capability". Similarly, he is not going to be deterred if you are unwilling or unable to talk to him, for if communications break down he will have no idea what it is you do not want him to do or what you are exactly threatening. Finally, if he is irrational or does not fear the loss of things you are threatening to destroy, he will be unable to make the cost-gain calculation and will not be deterred.

Nuclear strategies

These four points – credibility, capability, communications and rationality – are central to the process of nuclear deterrence, as can be seen by looking at nuclear strategy since 1945. For the first four years, until the Soviets tested their first atomic device in 1949, the Americans enjoyed a monopoly of atomic weapons, easily satisfying the four criteria; the destruction of Hiroshima and Nagasaki showed that they had both credibility and capability, the Soviets were clearly aware that the weapons existed and were rational enough not to tempt the Americans to use them against the Soviet Union. This one-sided situation began to change once the Soviets entered the "atomic club", but as they lacked the means to deliver their bombs onto American soil, no one in the United States feared atomic attack.

A more definite strategy began to emerge in the early 1950s, partly because of the advent of nuclear weapons with their enormous destructive potential, but also because events in both Europe and Korea had shown that American strength was not preventing the Soviets from threatening or supporting policies of communist expansion. They believed that low-level crises would never develop into nuclear confrontation.

In an effort to make the American position clear and so enhance deterrence, Eisenhower's Secretary of State, John Foster Dulles, introduced the strategy of "massive retaliation" in 1954, threatening the Soviets with instantaneous destruction of selected targets if they ever openly attacked NATO forces in Europe or American allies elsewhere. As only the United States had the capability to wage nuclear war, deterrence was strengthened.

The ultimate weapon: the distinctive mushroom cloud of an atomic explosion hangs in the sky over a test-site.

This began to be undermined in the late 1950s, for once the Soviets seemed to be developing missiles with the range to hit the United States, any attack on Soviet cities under massive retaliation would lead to counter-attacks against American population centres, and no one could really believe that the Americans would consciously commit suicide in that way. This was reinforced by the fact that massive retaliation was not triggered by the crises over Berlin in 1961 or Cuba a year later: in other words, the strategy lacked credibility.

In an effort to redress the balance, Kennedy's Secretary of State, Robert McNamara, announced a new strategy of "graduated deterrence" in 1963. In the event of a crisis, this policy offered a number of "options" for limited destruction short of full-scale nuclear war. If, for example, the Soviets carried out a limited attack on European targets, hoping to keep the level of aggression below that which would trigger massive retaliation, the Americans would be able to respond at that lower level, threatening the destruction of limited targets in the Soviet Union or other Warsaw Pact countries. This has remained the basis of American strategy into the 1980s, with the number and type of options under constant review.

The MAD strategy

As the two sides became more evenly matched in this way, they entered a situation known as "mutual assured destruction" – MAD for short – and this forms the central core of modern nuclear deterrence. It is based upon the ability of both sides to survive ("ride out") a nuclear attack and still have sufficient weapons left with which to inflict enormous damage on the enemy.

If, for example, the Soviets decided to attack the United States – to carry out what is known as a "first strike" – they would have to aim their missiles at targets they could see, namely the ICBMs in their specially hardened silos on American soil and the bases containing the B-1B and B-52 bombers. However successful this turned out to be (the Americans in the late 1970s were predicting the loss of over 90 per cent of their silos in such an attack), it would not be able to disarm the Americans entirely.

As soon as the attack took place, the surviving ICBMs and bombers, together with the submarine-launched missiles, immune to surprise attack because the submarines would be hiding in deep-ocean areas, would be launched against the Soviet Union in a retaliatory "second strike" of devastating power. In such circumstances, it would take a particularly irra-

tional leader actually to initiate a nuclear war, for whatever the cause of the conflict, he would be effectively committing suicide.

So long as this situation exists, the world is relatively safe from general nuclear war, but it does depend upon maintaining a balance of nuclear capability. The most obvious danger to stability lies in technology, for if one side should suddenly gain the means of protecting its land-based nuclear forces against a first strike or if the enemy should gain the means to destroy all elements of the "Triad" of land, sea and air launched weapons in one go, the balance would be upset and the country with the new advantage would not be deterred from using its forces.

In the late 1960s, there was widespread fear that improved accuracy of nuclear warheads would create such an imbalance, and although in this particular case the two sides kept pace with each other so that neither gained the advantage, the possibility remains.

Loading warheads on an American ICBM.

The more accurate the weapon, the more chance there is of destroying missile silos in a first strike: hence the development of "multiple independently targeted re-entry vehicles" (MIRVs), warheads which detach from the missile as it travels towards the enemy homeland and fall to hit precise and separate targets. This was made possible by new on-board computers which, once programmed, can guide the warhead into an area as small as 50 square metres.

Multiple warheads also increase the number of weapons that can be fired in a nuclear strike – most ICBMs now carry at least 10 MIRVs in place of the single warhead of 20 years ago – and this has led both sides to concentrate on improved protection as a counter. In the late 1960s, the trend was towards special anti-ballistic missile (ABM) systems using rockets to intercept the incoming warheads, but these were expensive and unlikely to destroy more than a fraction of the enemy force.

A US Minuteman III ICBM in its silo.

Star Wars

The ABM Treaty of 1972, restricting such systems to two sites only, seemed to ensure that neither side would gain the defensive advantage that would upset the balance. But this began to change when, on 23 March 1983, President Reagan announced his Strategic Defense Initiative (SDI) or "Star Wars" plan, for if this ever came into operation, any attack by the Soviets upon the United States would be destroyed before the warheads reached their targets.

Special satellites would monitor Soviet missile sites and, at the first sign of launch, would then alert space-based "battle stations" armed with laser-beam weapons or other devices capable of destroying the enemy forces as they flew above the Earth towards the United States. Reagan's declared intention was to create a situation in which a first strike would be impossible, so removing any temptation to use nuclear weapons at all. However, to the Soviets, the scheme was dangerously destabilising, for if the Americans felt secure behind their SDI screen, they might choose to launch a first strike which the Soviets could not answer.

In 1983, SDI seemed futuristic in the extreme, and there were doubts that even the Americans could produce a system capable of destroying an estimated 10,000 warheads in the short time it takes for ICBMs to travel from one superpower to the other. However research went ahead. As there was strong evidence that the Soviets were trying to match the technology involved, producing their own version of SDI, a highly

expensive "race" was already underway. Whoever won that race would gain an advantage which was guaranteed to destroy the balance of MAD.

A final area in which technology could cause problems would be a sudden breakthrough in anti-submarine warfare, for if one side gained the means to track the missile-carrying submarines of his enemy, he would be able to destroy them as part of a first strike. Under MAD, the submarines are crucial, containing the bulk of the second-strike forces available, so their loss in the early stages of a nuclear exchange would give the attacker the advantage he needed. It would be very difficult to deter someone who knew that he could completely disarm his enemy within the first few minutes of a war.

Nuclear proliferation

But the dangers are not all to do with technology. By the mid-1980s, it was generally accepted (although impossible to prove) that both Israel and South Africa had acquired nuclear weapons and that a number of other countries, including Argentina, Iraq and Pakistan, were very close to joining them. All these countries were involved in wars or potential conflicts – indeed, that was probably why they were interested in gaining nuclear capability – and it did not take much imagination to foresee local conflicts escalating to a nuclear level. If these involved allies of the superpowers, the latter might be forced to intervene, becoming involved in a situation already beyond the stage of deterrence.

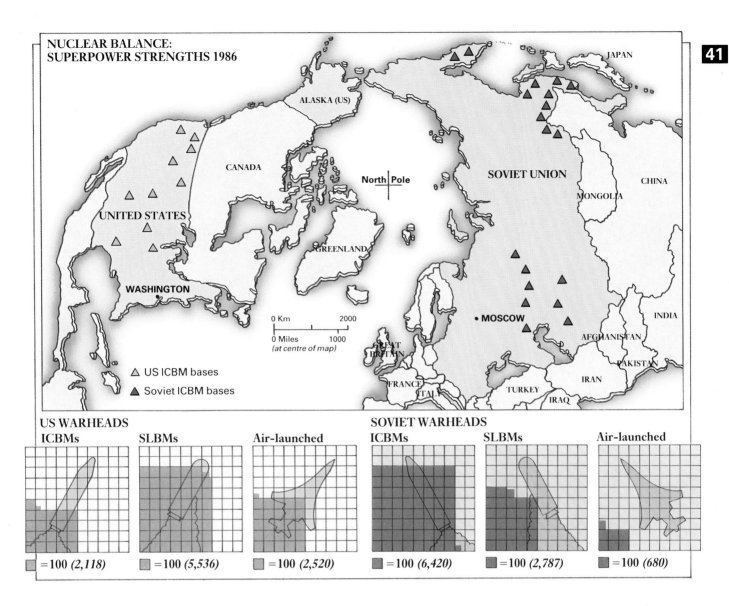

**NUCLEAR BALANCE:
SUPERPOWER STRENGTHS 1986**

ALASKA (US)

CANADA

North Pole

SOVIET UNION

CHINA

MONGOLIA

UNITED STATES

GREENLAND

WASHINGTON

0 Km   2000

0 Miles   1000
(at centre of map)

△ US ICBM bases

▲ Soviet ICBM bases

MOSCOW

INDIA

AFGHANISTAN

PAKISTAN

GREAT
BRITAIN

FRANCE
ITALY

TURKEY

IRAN

IRAQ

JAPAN

US WARHEADS

ICBMs	SLBMs	Air-launched
■ =100 *(2,118)*	■ =100 *(5,536)*	■ =100 *(2,520)*

SOVIET WARHEADS

ICBMs	SLBMs	Air-launched
■ =100 *(6,420)*	■ =100 *(2,787)*	■ =100 *(680)*

If, in addition, the new nuclear-capable countries were ruled by men who saw no reason to be deterred, either because they were irrational or did not fear the loss of cities or people, it would be very difficult to avoid a use of nuclear weapons. It would be extremely unlikely, for example, that any threat to destroy Tehran would deter the Ayatollah Khomeini of Iran: he would probably see it as a necessary sacrifice in the spread of Muslim fundamentalism, a sacrifice of people already convinced that death in battle guarantees them entry into Paradise.

Human error

There is one other way in which deterrence might fail, and it is perhaps the most worrying. In November 1979 data indicating a nuclear attack was fed into the computers at the American early warning headquarters deep inside a mountain at Colorado Springs. It was supposed to be for exercise purposes only, but the computers insisted that the attack was real. The Americans went onto the alert. Crews of B-52 bombers raced to their aircraft for takeoff, and in their underground silos the crews of the ICBMs began preliminary launch procedures. In June 1980, a faulty microchip again indicated a nuclear attack.

Both alarms lasted less than two minutes before American radars and satellites monitoring Soviet missile sites confirmed that there was no danger, but the fact that mistakes can happen must be worrying. Senior American officials insist that there are so many warning devices that individual faults in the systems will always be ironed out before the missiles are launched, but one only has to think what might have happened if such faults had occurred during a period of high tension between the superpowers to appreciate the danger. As the Soviets undoubtedly suffer the same sorts of errors or faults which the West does not know about, the chances of war by mistake are multiplied.

Thus, deterrence is by no means secure, being subject to all the pressures of technological change, irrationality and human error in a world where the number of nuclear-capable countries is likely to grow. In such circumstances, MAD is a very delicate balance and one that might not last indefinitely.

EAST VERSUS WEST: REAL OR IMAGINED THREATS

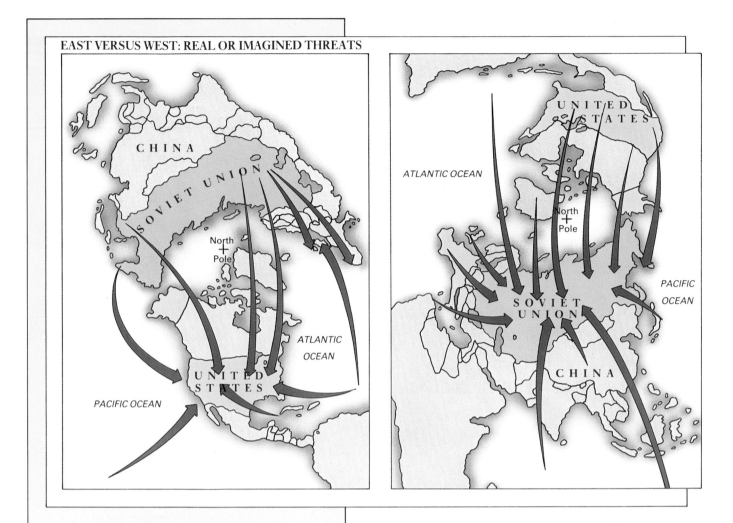

CHAPTER 4
NATO AND THE WARSAW PACT

The superpower confrontation is most obvious on the continent of Europe. Since 1955, when the Soviet Union created the Warsaw Pact partly in response to West Germany's entry into the NATO alliance, Europe has been divided into two heavily armed rival blocs. Both maintain huge armed forces, nuclear as well as conventional (non-nuclear), facing each other across the Inner-German Border (IGB) and on the "flanks" in Norway and Turkey. But neither alliance is perfect. Both NATO and the Warsaw Pact suffer from geographical, political and military weaknesses. The result is a stalemate which, ironically, makes Europe one of the least violent areas of the modern world, but the potential for war is frightening.

Europe has always been a centre for alliances. Throughout its history, the continent has contained countries which, fearing the intentions of their neighbours, have made military arrangements with other countries to ensure survival. Before 1939, the "balance of power" created by these alliances was always shifting and, as a result, wars were frequent. The alliances formed at the end of the Second World War, however, took on a more permanent form, reflecting the military and political reality of the Cold War. Since 1955, Europe has been divided into two rival camps, kept together by a combination of nuclear fear and ideological commitment.

NATO

The first of these to emerge was the North Atlantic Treaty Organisation (NATO) formed on 4 April 1949. It had its origins in the immediate aftermath of the Second World War, when Britain and France signed the Treaty of Dunkirk (4 March 1947), promising mutual support if either was attacked by a third party.

This was taken one stage further when the so-called Benelux countries (Belgium, the Netherlands and Luxembourg) were added to the alliance through the Treaty of Brussels (13 March 1948).

But with the emergence of a perceived Soviet threat to the security of western Europe, shown most clearly by the Berlin Blockade of 1948-49, it was obvious that something more solid and wide-ranging was needed, preferably based on the strength of the United States, with its atomic capability. The result was the NATO alliance, signed by a total of 12 like-minded countries – Belgium, Britain, Canada, Denmark, France, Iceland, Italy, Luxembourg, the Netherlands, Norway, Portugal and the United States.

Since that time, other members have been added. In 1952, both Greece and Turkey, fearful of Soviet policies towards southern Europe, signed the treaty documents; in 1955 West Germany was welcomed into the alliance and in 1982 Spain brought the total up to 16 member states. Not all members are fully committed – in 1966 France left the military structure in protest at the introduction of a new NATO strategy, and Greece followed suit between 1974 and 1980 when the other members did nothing to stop the Turkish invasion of Cyprus. However in general terms, NATO has remained a remarkably coherent collection of independent states dedicated to protecting each other in the event of an attack on one of the members.

The Warsaw Pact

The Warsaw Pact, signed on 14 May 1955, is a different type of alliance, formed to ensure the continued dominance of the Soviet Union over eastern Europe. Between 1945 and 1955, the Soviets controlled the "satellite" states through force of arms alone, creating the "buffer zone" against attack from the west.

But there were limits to Soviet power to match an expanding NATO and contain growing unrest in the eastern bloc. When the Austrian State Treaty (15 May 1955) forced them to withdraw some troops from the region, the Soviets used the situation to rethink their future role, allowing the eastern states to take over some of the responsibility for their own defence.

To guarantee continued Soviet control, the Warsaw Pact was created, involving Albania, Bulgaria, Czechoslovakia, Hungary, Poland, Romania and the Soviet Union, with East Germany as an "observer" until the end of 1955, when she too became a full member. Since then, Albania has left the Pact, in protest at the invasion of Czechoslovakia in 1968, and Romania has ceased to take a full part in Pact affairs.

At the same time, however, the Soviets have shown a willingness to maintain their control over both Hungary and Czechoslovakia by force of arms, reinforcing the general feeling in the West that, in the central parts of the Pact at least, the Soviet Union is prepared to go to considerable lengths to ensure continued domination.

The Warsaw Pact: a parade of Soviet weapons is held every year in Moscow in October to celebrate the 1917 revolution.

The balance of terror

As part of their respective structures, both alliances station large armed forces in Europe on a permanent basis, with the potential to reinforce them with even greater numbers of men and weapons in the event of a crisis or war. Most of these forces face each other across the Inner-German Border (IGB), helping to create a "flashpoint" of terrifying potential. Any clash of interests or minor conflict between rival camps anywhere along the IGB would almost be guaranteed to escalate into war, and the same could happen on one of the two "flanks", either in northern Norway or northern Turkey.

The fact that this has not yet occurred is perhaps surprising, given the fluctuating state of superpower relations, and there is no doubt that the development of nuclear forces by both sides, deterring the "enemy" from pursuing policies which might escalate into war, has done much to maintain peace, but there is more to it than that. The fact that neither alliance is strong enough to dominate Europe entirely has produced a stalemate of some stability. An examination of the two alliances in terms of strengths and weaknesses will illustrate the point.

NATO derives its greatest strength from the fact that it is an alliance of independent, like-minded countries which choose to join together against what they see as a potential enemy. This is reflected in the orga-nisation of the alliance, for within the North Atlantic Council and its subsidiary military and political committees all decisions have to be made by consensus (everyone agreeing). Individual members cannot be forced to accept ideas they do not like.

This means, in turn, that every member enjoys the same amount of influence, regardless of its size or military strength. Thus a country like Iceland, with no armed forces of its own, can in theory stop policies put forward by the United States, even if, in reality, the latter is dominant in political, economic and military terms. Similarly, countries like France and Greece have been able to withdraw from the military (but not the political) structure of NATO without breaking up the alliance itself.

But weaknesses do exist. The most important concerns the geography of the alliance, for the 16 member states do not form a solid land bloc within which a co-ordinated defence can emerge. In the event of a war with the Warsaw Pact, NATO will depend very heavily indeed upon the industrial and military strength of the United States. Yet that country lies 4,800 km (3,000 miles) away from the likely area of fighting, across an immense ocean that will contain Soviet submarines and surface ships.

Even within Europe, the geography of the alliance is poor, posing difficult problems. If the Warsaw Pact should attack across the IGB, for example, NATO

NATO troops patrol the Inner-German Border.

A NATO council meeting.

forces in West Germany would have very little "depth" of territory to fall back in and, if France should remain outside the military structure, the situation would be even worse. If, on the other hand, the attack should come on the flanks, NATO faces an even greater problem of co-ordination: in the north, the narrowness of Norwegian territory leaves no room for manoeuvre, while in the south, the five member states – Portugal, Spain, Italy, Greece and Turkey – are separated one from the other or isolated by the sheer distances involved. The existence of the so-called "neutrality gap", created by the presence of the neutral, non-NATO states of Austria and Switzerland, does nothing to help, forming a wedge of territory that physically splits the southern tier of countries from those of central Europe.

Political tensions

Nor is the weakness purely one of terrain, for NATO also suffers political strains. In the past, the decision by France to follow a separate military line showed deep divisions between the member states, although in this case the problem was absorbed without doing too much damage. The same has not been true of the split between Greece and Turkey.

This came to a head over Cyprus in 1974, when the Turkish government, concerned that Turkish-Cypriot citizens were about to be overwhelmed by Greek-Cypriot extremists, ordered an invasion of the island and took over the northern region. Since then, relations between Greece and Turkey have deteriorated to the point where the two countries refuse to co-operate even in NATO affairs. As they are also in dispute over

mineral exploration rights in the Aegean Sea, an area dominated by Greece through the territorial waters around its islands, some of which lie virtually on the Turkish coast, the chances of NATO solidarity there are slim.

At a less dramatic but equally worrying level, relations between the United States and her European allies have often been strained. To a large extent, this stems from a difference of opinion about the purpose of NATO, for the Americans tend to see it as an anti-communist alliance whereas to the Europeans it is more specifically anti-Russian.

This has led the Americans on occasions to demand much more European involvement in policies designed to "contain" the spread of communism outside the NATO area – notably in Vietnam in the 1960s – only to face rejection by European countries concerned that such policies are diverting American resources away from the defence of Europe itself. As many Americans already believe that the Europeans are not contributing enough in terms of money and armed forces to their own defence, depending far too much on the United States, the development of mistrust is likely.

The nuclear umbrella

In the early days of the alliance, when the Americans adopted the straightforward policy of "massive retaliation", threatening to use nuclear weapons in response to any Soviet aggression in Europe, the Europeans felt safe, sheltering beneath the American "nuclear umbrella", but as the Soviets gained the capability to hit back at American cities, the situation had to change.

The American adoption of "graduated deterrence", in which a number of options short of full-scale nuclear attack were introduced, undoubtedly enhanced deterrence between the superpowers, but it left the Europeans feeling vulnerable. Their view was that in the event of Soviet attack across the IGB, there was no longer any guarantee that the Americans would respond with nuclear weapons, and if the Soviets realised this, they would not be deterred from making such attacks in the future. Indeed, apparent lack of nuclear protection was the main reason for the French withdrawal from the military structure and the subsequent French development of an independent nuclear force, capable of carrying out its own "massive retaliation".

Flexible response – defence and deterrence
Among the other NATO allies, the crisis was averted by the introduction of a new strategy in 1967. Known as "flexible response", this was an attempt to satisfy the American desire for an alternative to national suicide while maintaining the defence of Europe to the satisfaction of the European allies.

If, for example, the Warsaw Pact should attack using purely conventional forces, NATO will respond at exactly the same level (a policy of defence) while threatening to use nuclear weapons if the attack persists (a policy of deterrence). As this process can be adapted to fit almost any level of initial attack – if the Soviets begin with nuclear strikes in Europe, NATO will respond with retaliatory strikes against the Warsaw Pact while threatening to use nuclear weapons against the Soviet homeland if the attacks persist – the strategy is both flexible and appropriate, but it has not quietened fears within the alliance.

To the Americans, the strategy will only work if the Europeans are willing to increase the size of their conventional forces and to fight a conventional war – something which they are clearly reluctant to do – while to the Europeans, the American reluctance to use nuclear weapons straight away implies a lack of commitment to the security of Europe. Current trends towards the development of technology as an alternative to high force levels, producing weapons which can impose enormous casualties on Warsaw Pact attackers and so redress the balance, might solve the problem, but as this will be expensive, the Europeans are less than enthusiastic. The controversies continue.

But it would be wrong to imagine that the Warsaw Pact is some huge military monster, ready to exploit such NATO weaknesses in a display of unstoppable force,

for it too has its problems. There can be no doubt that, in numerical terms, the Pact is strong – taken overall, it outnumbers NATO in tanks, artillery pieces, aircraft and other conventional equipment by a ratio of about 2:1 – and it could be argued that Soviet domination in both political and military affairs gives the alliance a cohesion that NATO lacks, but this is a superficial analysis. Only when the weaknesses of the Warsaw Pact are recognised can we get a more accurate picture of the balance between the superpower blocs in Europe.

Warsaw Pact weaknesses
The first, and most important, of these weaknesses stems from the nature of the Pact itself for, unlike NATO, it owes its origins to the policies of one state only – the Soviet Union. The other member states are not "independent", having been forced to accept the creation of the Pact in 1955 for reasons that were not necessarily in their interests. Admittedly, one of the original members has managed to leave the alliance structure and others have tried, with varying degrees of success, to distance themselves from the policies imposed by the Soviet Union. But they have only got away with this because their countries are difficult to invade from the east.

Albania, for example, has no common border with other Warsaw Pact countries, so her decision to take an independent line in 1968 could not be countered by Soviet troops on her soil. Other countries have not been so fortunate, as events in Hungary in 1956 and Czechoslovakia in 1968 go to prove, and the fact that the Soviets have felt it necessary to impose their views by force of arms on these two occasions shows that, in the end, it is Moscow that dictates the policies of the Pact. When it is borne in mind that of the eight original members of the Pact, only one (Bulgaria) has shown no signs of opposing those policies since 1955, any idea of alliance solidarity seems false.

Resentment about Soviet control of Pact affairs does not mean, of course, that the East European armies would refuse to fight in the event of a war – all are closely geared to the ideals of communism and, as events in Poland since 1980 have proved, they tend to remain loyal to the existing governments – but there can be no guarantees that the Pact will survive the pressures of a major crisis, particularly if the Soviets seem to be losing. There are too many people in the East who would welcome a weakening of Soviet power for Moscow to risk provoking a crisis or war at the superpower level.

Nor is such a weakening of power unlikely, for in purely military terms, the Pact suffers from certain key disadvantages. Although the seven surviving members form a solid territorial bloc in Europe, with no oceans or "neutrality gaps" to expose their flanks, that bloc is not ideally placed in the superpower balance. NATO can contain the Pact by preventing its naval forces from breaking out into the oceans of the world – the exits from the Baltic through the Skaggerat and from the Black Sea through the Bosphorus Straits are dominated by NATO countries, while any movement into the North Atlantic from Murmansk can be monitored by NATO aircraft and surface ships.

Although the Soviet Navy has increased dramatically in size since the 1950s, this remains a major problem. Even within the territorial bloc itself, communications continue to be poor by Western standards, delaying the movement of troops or the mobilisation of reserves, while the threat to the Soviet Union from China unavoidably diverts significant Soviet forces from the European theatre.

Finally, if it should ever come to a shooting war, the Warsaw Pact may have to depend upon sheer weight of numbers to defeat the NATO armies. The West still retains a substantial advantage in terms of weapons technology, deploying better tanks, missiles and aircraft than the majority of the Pact members, and although the "technology gap" may be closing, the Western development of Emerging Technology (ET) promises new weapons which the Pact will be hard-pressed to match. In the end it would be a fight between quantity and quality, with neither side guaranteed success.

Thus, in political, geographical and military terms, the two sides are effectively "balanced out". NATO may have fewer armed forces available, but they are of better quality and enjoy a greater kill capability; the Warsaw Pact may give a greater impression of coherence, but NATO is able to absorb its differences more easily; NATO may be split by oceans and "neutrality gaps", but the Warsaw Pact is more easily contained within its existing boundaries; NATO members may have gone their own way occasionally, but only the Warsaw Pact has actually lost a member state entirely. The result is a stalemate in which huge armed forces face each other in a manifestation of Cold War politics: the potential for war is enormous, but the chances of it developing are kept in check. That is what the Cold War is all about.

Afghanistan 1985: while the superpowers face each other in the New Cold War, many suffer from the effects of actual fighting.

CONFLICT IN THE 20TH CENTURY : APPENDICES

The tensions between East and West take many forms. Around the world there are a number of "flashpoints", each capable of bursting into conflict, and none is more potentially explosive than the Central Front in Europe, where NATO and Warsaw Pact forces maintain an uneasy balance. Elsewhere, rivalries exist in Space and both superpower blocs, led by politicians of strong personality and beliefs, devote enormous energies to gathering information on their rivals.

PERSONALITIES

Leonid Ilyich Brezhnev (1906-1982). Soviet Premier, 1964-82. After political experience in the Ukraine and Moldavia, he became a member of the Soviet Politburo in 1957, succeeding Nikita Khrushchev as First Secretary of the Communist Party in 1964. He developed the Brezhnev Doctrine, claiming a Soviet right to interfere in neighbouring countries if communism seemed threatened, and ordered Warsaw Pact troops into Czechoslovakia (1968) and Afghanistan (1979). He signed the SALT I (1972) and SALT II (1979) agreements with the United States.

James ("Jimmy") Carter (1924-   ). Democratic President of the United States, 1976-80. He was elected Governor of Georgia in 1971 and then US President in November 1976. Dedicated to re-establishing US presidential power in the aftermath of the Vietnam War and Watergate, he pursued policies of detente with the Soviet Union based upon the principles of human rights. He negotiated a peace agreement between Egypt and Israel (1978), but failed to maintain his popularity at home. He was defeated by Reagan in the presidential election of November 1980.

Sir Winston Churchill (1874-1965). British politician, historian and writer. He entered politics in 1900, beginning a remarkable career which led to his appointment as Prime

Leonid Brezhnev.

Mikhail Gorbachev.

Minister from 1940-45. Despite his crucial role in sustaining British resolve during the Second World War, he was defeated at the general election of July 1945. He returned as Prime Minister in 1951, dedicated to close relations with the United States in the Cold War, but was forced to resign through ill health in 1955.

Alexander Dubček (1921-   ). Czechoslovak Communist leader, 1967-69. He tried to introduce reforms of a liberal nature in April 1968, helping to trigger a Soviet/Warsaw Pact invasion of his country in August. He was replaced as Party leader in 1969 and subsequently disgraced.

Mikhail Gorbachev (1930-   ). Soviet First Secretary, 1985-   . He is one of the first of a new generation of Soviet leaders who did not take part in the Great Patriotic War (1941-45). He became Soviet leader on the death of Konstantin Chernenko in March 1985. He has adopted a more conciliatory line towards the West, offering arms control concessions and nuclear weapons "freezes", although his long-term intentions are unclear.

Sergei Gorshkov (1910-   ). Commander-in-Chief of the Soviet Navy, 1956-85. After service in the Great Patriotic War, he was given the task of modernising the Soviet Navy by Khrushchev in 1956. He succeeded brilliantly, building up a balanced, ocean-going fleet of submarines and surface ships which could challenge the US Navy almost anywhere on the high seas.

John ("Jack") Kennedy (1917-1963). Democratic President of the United States, 1960-63. Coming from an influential East Coast family, it was natural for him to enter politics. He served as Senator for Massachusetts (1952-60) and defeated Nixon in the presidential election of November 1960. Initially regarded as too young and inexperienced for international politics, he proved his skill during the Cuban Missile Crisis of October 1962. He was assassinated in November 1963.

Nikita Sergeyevich Khrushchev (1894-1971). Soviet Premier, 1958-64. He joined the Soviet Communist Party in 1918 and progressed steadily up the political ladder, eventually replacing Stalin as First Secretary on the latter's death in March 1953. He ruled jointly with Nikolai Bulganin until 1958, then on his own. A ruthless man, he engaged in "brinkmanship" policies with the United States, culminating in the Cuban Missile Crisis of October 1962, in which he was forced to back down. He was removed from office in October 1964.

Richard Nixon (1913-). Republican President of the United States, 1968-74. He served as Dwight Eisenhower's vice-president (1952-

John Kennedy.

60) before being defeated by Kennedy in the presidential election of November 1960. However, he was elected President in November 1968 and re-elected four years later. He was responsible for negotiating the SALT I agreement with the Soviet Union (1972) and for pulling US troops out of Vietnam (1973), but was forced to resign in August 1974 over the Watergate affair.

Ronald Reagan (1911-). Republican President of the United States, 1980- . After a career in film acting he entered politics, being

elected Governor of California in 1966. He defeated Carter in the presidential election of November 1980 and was re-elected four years later. He has taken a much tougher line than his predecessor in relations with the Soviet Union, condemning Soviet actions in Afghanistan and Central America.

Harry Truman (1884-1972). Democratic President of the United States, 1945-52. Chosen as Franklin Roosevelt's vice-president in 1944, he took over the presidency on Roosevelt's death in April 1945. He was elected in his own right in November 1948. An early advocate of policies to prevent the spread of communism (the Truman Doctrine), he took the United States into NATO (1949) and committed US troops to the defence of South Korea (1950).

Lech Walesa (1943-). Polish trade union activist. Employed as an electrician in the Lenin Shipyard, Gdansk, he was Chairman of the Strike Committee during the troubles of 1970. Sacked in 1976, he re-emerged four years later as a driving force behind the creation of the independent trade union "Solidarity". He was detained in 1981, and was awarded the Nobel Peace Prize in 1983.

Richard Nixon.

Ronald Reagan.

Lech Walesa.

EAST-WEST FLASHPOINTS

Since 1945, the world has been dominated by the actions and intentions of the superpowers. The influence, power and military strength of the United States and Soviet Union have remained roughly in balance, but this does not mean that the world is safe. Throughout the globe there are areas in which superpower interests clash, producing friction and potential danger of war. Such areas are aptly dubbed "flashpoints", on the understanding that any crisis in them could quite easily lead to full-scale superpower hostility, with all its awesome implications.

The Inner-German Border (IGB) When the Second World War ended in 1945, huge armies faced each other along a line stretching from just east of Lübeck on the Baltic coast down to the Austrian border. Germany was split between the Soviets to the east of this line and the Western allies to the west: it is a line

that has persisted to the present day. Until the late 1960s, a Soviet (later Warsaw Pact) advance across the line was seen as the most likely cause of superpower war and NATO maintained its forces accordingly.

With the gradual acceptance of European borders and evolution of effective policies of deterrence, the danger has subsided in more recent years. Nevertheless, the Group of Soviet Forces Germany (GSFG), comprising a Guards Tank Army and its support units, is readily available for assaults across the IGB and the chances of a surprise attack still persist. The defence of this area is the major concern of NATO, and West Germany, the United States, Britain, Belgium, the Netherlands and Canada all maintain forces there as a deterrent.

Berlin
The decision to divide Berlin between the victorious allies in 1945 was probably meant to be a

temporary arrangement only, and to the West it must have seemed absurd to maintain an enclave inside the Eastern bloc, surrounded by potentially hostile territory. But continued Western presence in Berlin became a matter of prestige in 1948-49, when the Soviets tried to force the West to withdraw, so forces remain in place.

To prevent unnecessary provocation, West Berlin is treated as a separate entity – it is not part of the Federal Republic (West Germany) and the Western troops there are not part of NATO – and theoretically the post-war *Kommandatura* (four-power ruling authority) still exists, although without a Soviet representative. An incident along the Berlin Wall or at one of the checkpoints could blow up into a major crisis, and any renewed attempt by the East to impose a blockade of Western sectors would probably be met with a strong response.

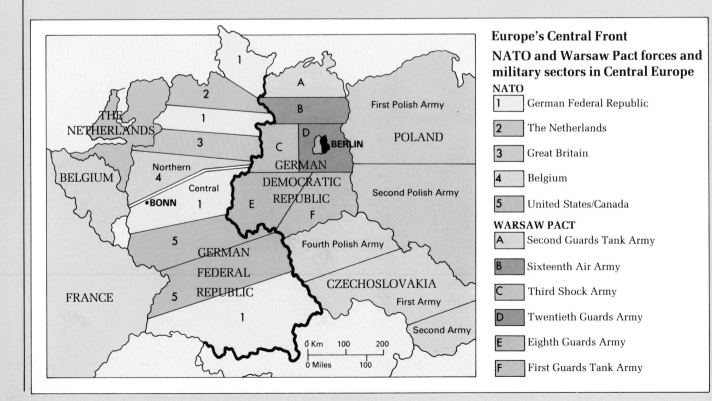

Europe's Central Front

NATO and Warsaw Pact forces and military sectors in Central Europe

NATO

1	German Federal Republic
2	The Netherlands
3	Great Britain
4	Belgium
5	United States/Canada

WARSAW PACT

A	Second Guards Tank Army
B	Sixteenth Air Army
C	Third Shock Army
D	Twentieth Guards Army
E	Eighth Guards Army
F	First Guards Tank Army

Yugoslavia

Because Yugoslavia has always taken an independent line in the communist camp, it occupies a peculiar position in the "no-man's-land" between East and West. Comprising a number of states and autonomous provinces, each with its own ethnic and political ideas, the country is ripe for civil unrest if the central authority should ever fail.

For a long time, the aftermath of Tito's death seemed a likely occasion for an East-West clash. Many felt that it was largely his influence that held the country together, but his death in 1980 passed without crisis. The country is now less of a flashpoint, but if the Yugoslav government lost control, the Soviets might be tempted (or asked by more hardline communists) to step in, forcing the West to react to prevent a spread of Soviet influence into the Adriatic.

The Middle East

The main source of conflict in the Middle East – that between Israel and her Arab neighbours – has been kept in check since 1948 by the two superpowers maintaining a balance through their respective allies. So long as American backing for Israel and Soviet support for at least some of the "front-line" Arab states (currently Syria and Iraq) persist, and neither side comes close to destroying the other entirely, all should be safe in global terms.

However, if the balance is upset – if, for example, Israel seems about to be overrun or if Israeli forces approach the capital of Syria (as occurred in October 1973) – then the superpowers may feel obliged to intervene, with obvious consequences.

A similar situation exists in the Arabian (Persian) Gulf, where Iran and Iraq have been fighting since 1980. Although the division of superpower support in the region is less clear-cut, the consequences of a shift in the balance of power could be catastrophic.

If Iran seemed about to collapse, for example, the Soviets might step in to occupy territory (to protect Afghanistan), so triggering an American move to safeguard the vital oilfields; if Iraq was threatened, the Soviets might step in to protect an ally, with similar results.

Central America

The spread of communism into the Caribbean and Central America is a particular nightmare of the United States. Caught by surprise by the success of Fidel Castro in Cuba (1959), Washington has since gone to great lengths to prevent what it sees as a Moscow-controlled plot to deny the West access to the Panama Canal and the resources of Latin America.

The success of the Sandinistas in Nicaragua (1979) and the communist threat to El Salvador have forced the Americans to act, giving military and economic support to anti-communist groups or governments in the region, even, on occasion, sending their own troops into action, as in Grenada (1983).

The future

Other flashpoints undoubtedly exist – since 1953, for example, rival forces, backed by East and West, have maintained a very precarious peace on the 38th parallel in Korea – and yet more may well arise in the future. The only hope lies in the fact that, in more than 40 years, the world has not been plunged into global war.

Government troops search a village for guerrillas in the bitter civil war in El Salvador, 1982.

EAST-WEST BALANCE OF FORCES

In the event of a full-scale war between NATO and the Warsaw Pact in Europe, the fighting would probably progress through a number of phases in a process known as "escalation". To begin with, both sides would try to avoid the use of nuclear weapons, concentrating instead upon their conventional (non-nuclear) ground, air and naval forces to gain their objectives.

So far as NATO is concerned, it will deploy its forces to defend its territory, reacting to any Warsaw Pact attack across the East-West border. During this phase of the war, the numbers of military units (usually counted in terms of divisions), tanks, artillery pieces, ships, submarines and aircraft will be crucial, but the balance is by no means straightforward.

Naval forces

Although the balance of naval forces favours NATO, it should be borne in mind that countries such as the United States, Britain and France have global interests which may take some of their naval units away from the North Atlantic. During the Falklands War (1982), for example, Britain was forced to deploy nearly two-thirds of her surface fleet to the

NATO-Warsaw Pact Conventional Forces, 1986		NATO	Warsaw Pact
1 Naval Forces	Surface Ships	366	220
	Submarines	190	217
	Naval Aircraft	1950	1100
2 Land and Air Forces	Divisions	55	105
	Tanks	10,000	28,000
	Artillery	4750	17,500
	Aircraft	2500	4750

(Figures taken from the *Defence White Paper* (UK) of May 1986; French and Spanish forces included in NATO totals)

South Atlantic, far away from NATO defensive areas. Equally, the Soviet Union is still engaged in substantial shipbuilding, so may catch up in time.

Even so, with Soviet naval forces effectively "bottled up" in the Baltic and Black Seas, the fighting would be confined largely to the Atlantic where NATO navies, organised and equipped to protect convoys from North America against air, surface and submarine attack, are in a marginally better position.

The European theatre
The same is not the case in Europe itself, for the land and air force

balance lies firmly in favour of the Warsaw Pact in numerical terms. Here, NATO would have to fight any conventional battle with considerable skill. The Warsaw Pact attack would probably follow the pattern of *Blitzkrieg* ("lightning war"), with massive air and ground forces searching for weaknesses in NATO's front line and having found them, rushing through in overwhelming numbers.

But NATO does enjoy two advantages, not shown in the table. First, the West would be on the defensive on familiar ground and, as most strategists agree that an attacker needs at least a 3:1 advantage in numbers to succeed, the Warsaw Pact would still have to concentrate its forces at predictable points. Second, NATO has the technological edge, producing weapons of superior quality and survivability (although there are signs that the East is catching up).

With both these advantages, it is logical for NATO to adopt a strategy which involves the destruction of Warsaw Pact forces as they concentrate for the assault, using high technology, long-range weapons to hit enemy rear areas – in other words, the doctrine of FOFA (Follow On Forces Attack), adopted as a long-term planning guideline in 1984.

Aircraft on board the nuclear-powered carrier USS Dwight D. Eisenhower.

Nuclear weapons

If the Warsaw Pact should break through, however, NATO may be forced to resort to nuclear weapons as the next phase of escalation. To begin with, these would be tactical or battlefield weapons such as the Lance surface-to-surface missile or M-110 artillery piece firing nuclear shells. But if the war goes on, other nuclear systems could be used.

At a "theatre", or intermediate, level, in which nuclear weapons would be sent against targets in Europe only, systems such as the GLCM (ground launched cruise missile) – of the type currently deployed at Greenham Common airbase in England – or the Soviet SS-20 would appear.

Strategic weapons

Once the fighting had progressed this far, it would be virtually impossible to stop the escalation to "strategic" nuclear exchanges, in which ICBMs (intercontinental ballistic missiles), SLBMs (submarine launched ballistic

Strategic Nuclear Forces, 1986		USA	Soviet Union
ICBMs	Numbers of Missiles	1018	1398
	Numbers of Warheads	2118	6420
SLBMs	Numbers of Missiles	616	979
	Numbers of Warheads	5536	2787
Long-Range Bombers	Numbers of Aircraft	180	170
	Numbers of Nuclear Weapons	2520	680

(Figures taken from the IISS *Military Balance, 1985-1986*)

missiles) and long-range bombers such as the American B-1B or Soviet Backfire – all armed with numbers of nuclear weapons or warheads – would hit targets in the rival superpower homeland.

In strategic nuclear terms, the Americans deploy larger numbers of warheads on board submarines and bombers, while the Soviets have concentrated more on land-based ICBMs. To many, this implies that the Soviets are preparing for a "first strike" on the US homeland, sending ICBMs against missile silos in an

attempt to disarm the Americans (hence President Reagan's emphasis on a defensive system – Star Wars – to prevent Soviet success).

The Americans, by comparison, are ready to absorb (or destroy) such a strike, while keeping SLBMs and bombers available for a devastating "second (or retaliatory) strike". So long as that rough balance persists, with neither side in a position to "win", deterrence will hopefully prevail to prevent war. If it does not, the world as we know it would cease to exist.

A Tomahawk GLCM (ground launched cruise missile) is test-fired in Utah.

SPIES AND SPYING

Since the Second World War, both superpowers (and their respective allies) have gone to great lengths to gather information about the weapons and intentions of their rivals. In the United States, the CIA (Central Intelligence Agency) was set up in 1947, and in 1954 the Soviets responded by creating the KGB (*Komitet Gosudarstvennoi Bezopasnosti*, or Committee for State Security). In Britain the equivalent body is the Secret Intelligence Service (SIS), more commonly known as MI6. In all cases, the main tasks of the intelligence organisations are to monitor their opposite numbers in the East or West, to prevent "leakages" of information from their own side and to indulge in the age-old habit of spying.

The hardware

Information on a potential enemy can be gathered from a variety of sources. Since 1956, the United States has conducted high-altitude spying missions, using aircraft such as the U-2 (an example of which, piloted by Gary Powers, was shot down over Sverdlovsk on 1 May 1960) or the SR-71 "Blackbird". The Soviets have used Tu-20 "Bear" bombers, converted to the reconnaissance role, chiefly over Western Europe.

Such aircraft can provide good-quality aerial photographs of enemy weapons sites, but they are vulnerable to interception. Both sides, therefore, add to their intelligence picture by means of special "listening posts", capable of monitoring radio traffic (the British example is the Government Communications Headquarters – GCHQ – at Cheltenham), and with spy satellites, programmed to fly in orbits designed to take them over key locations. The infra-red, high-

Tupolev Tu-20s have been used over Western Europe.

definition satellite photographs can show remarkable detail: for example, the Americans have recently discovered a new Soviet aircraft carrier under construction using their "spy-in-the-sky".

Spy networks

But there are limits to such methods, and if either side wants to know what its rival is planning or how much it knows, it still turns to traditional spies – special agents infiltrated into the enemy camp to gather detailed information. Since 1945, such spy networks have enjoyed mixed success, although from the evidence available (which

can only be based upon those networks that have actually been discovered), it would seem that the Soviets have managed to infiltrate the very highest ranks of selected Western countries.

This was obvious as soon as the Second World War ended, for as the West became fearful of Soviet ambitions in Europe, a variety of spy rings were uncovered, principally in the atomic field. In 1946, a British physicist, Dr Alan Nunn May, who had worked on atomic research, was caught spying for the Soviet Union (he is known to have provided Moscow with examples of the uranium used in atomic weapons).

Lockheed SR-71 Blackbirds were used over Vietnam in the 1960s.

Four years later, in a much more worrying episode, Dr Klaus Fuchs was arrested. A German scientist who had fled from Hitler's regime in the late 1930s, Fuchs had worked on the atomic bomb project in the United States and had helped to set up Britain's Atomic Research facility at Harwell. He was sentenced to 14 years in prison for passing crucial information about bomb design to Moscow and his arrest threatened to expose other spies in Britain.

In 1951 Guy Burgess and Donald Maclean, officials in the Foreign Office, fled to the Soviet Union rather than face arrest. In the United States, Julius and Ethel Rosenberg were caught passing information to the Soviets at much the same time: they were found guilty and executed.

Other spy rings followed. In June 1957 Rudolf Ivanovich Abel (alias Martin Collins, but actually called William Fischer) was uncovered in Brooklyn, New York, where he had been acting as a "masterspy" since at least 1948, running a network of agents throughout the United States. His apartment was found to contain a short-wave radio transmitter,

Dr Klaus Fuchs, an "atom spy".

cypher pads for sending coded messages and microfilms – all the traditional "tools" of the spying trade.

British spies

Four years later in Britain, George Blake – a man who had been working within the SIS – was accused of betraying an unspecified number of Western agents operating behind the Iron Curtain. The so-

called "Navy Ring", run by Gordon Lonsdale and Peter and Helen Kroger, was also uncovered. The latter was responsible for gaining secret information from the Royal Navy's Underwater Weapons Establishment through Harry Houghton, who had been blackmailed into betraying his country.

By the early 1960s, therefore, key elements of the West's establishment seemed to be suspect in security terms, and subsequent events did little to alter this impression. In January 1963 Kim Philby – widely regarded as the "third man" in the Foreign Office spy ring – defected to the East, and rumours began of an even more dramatic infiltration by agents working for the Soviets.

In 1980 these came into the open when Anthony Blunt, then the Queen's art adviser, was accused of having acted as a spy while working for British Intelligence during the Second World War.

Defectors from the East

But spying has not been entirely one-sided. In 1962, for example, Colonel Oleg Penkovsky was arrested in Moscow and executed for passing secrets to the West. At the same time, a number of important intelligence people have defected from the East, providing invaluable information to their interrogators. The first was Igor Gouzenko, a cypher clerk in the Soviet embassy in Ottawa, who defected in 1945: his information probably exposed May, Fuchs and the Rosenbergs. In 1960 Anatoli Golitsyn, a Polish intelligence officer, defected after acting as a spy for the West for at least 18 months, and his information may have uncovered Blake and the Navy Ring.

Recently there have been a number of spies detected in the United States, including John Walker and members of his family.

Spying is a murky business, not at all like the glamorous image created by certain authors and film-makers. In fact, with satellites, aircraft and sophisticated listening posts now available, the age of the traditional spy may be over.

Ethel and Julius Rosenberg in custody in 1951.

THE SPACE RACE

On 4 October 1957, the Soviet Union surprised the world by successfully launching Sputnik I, the first artificial satellite to orbit the Earth. In technological terms, it was a major feat, but to the Americans it seemed to confirm their worst fears. Only two months previously a Soviet test-launch of a long-range rocket had suggested that it would not be long before the United States was threatened by nuclear-armed ICBMs (intercontinental ballistic missiles); Sputnik implied that such rockets were capable of operation far sooner than expected. Many Americans feared the creation of a "missile gap" in which the United States would be at a distinct disadvantage and, for the first time in history, vulnerable to direct enemy attack.

In reality, such a gap did not exist, but subsequent Soviet space achievements did nothing to calm the fears. In 1959, the Soviet unmanned spacecraft Luna II landed on the surface of the Moon, and on 12 April 1961 Yuri Gagarin became the first human being to leave the Earth's atmosphere, conducting a successful orbit before being recovered safely. This was too much for the Americans, who resolved not merely to match but to surpass the Soviet achievements. In 1961, President Kennedy authorised funds for a US space programme. The Cold War between the superpowers had entered a new dimension.

Why did it happen?

The superpower rivalry in space is not difficult to understand. In a confrontation like the Cold War, where actual fighting is avoided, the two sides will try to score points off each other by means of propaganda designed to portray their particular political system as superior to that of the enemy. This is done mainly for domestic consumption but is valuable in terms of persuading

Yuri Gagarin, the first cosmonaut.

other countries (particularly Third World countries in the 1960s) to support either East or West. At the same time, as the American reaction to Sputnik implies, any achievements in space can have military spin-offs to offer.

The Americans did not lag behind in the race for long. Less than a month after Gagarin's epic flight, Alan Shepard became the first American to leave the Earth's atmosphere, although it was to take until 20 February 1962 for John Glenn to achieve the first American orbit. Even then, the Soviets kept producing surprises: on 16 June 1963 Valentina Tereshkova became the first woman in space, carrying out 48 orbits of the Earth before returning to be feted as a "Heroine of the Soviet Union". The Americans still had some way to go to catch up; a process not aided by the fact that, of the first 35 space-probe launches, 19 failed to achieve their objectives.

The first man on the Moon

By 1963, however, the superpowers were estimated to be about "neck-and-neck" in the space race, and thereafter the Americans forged ahead. Their programme culminated in July 1969 when Neil Armstrong stepped onto the surface of the Moon, at the end of a flight described by President Nixon as "the greatest week in the history of the world since the Creation". It was a major achievement, dependent for success on the unrivalled expertise of American scientists, particularly in the exceptionally difficult field of

US astronauts meet Soviet cosmonauts in space on 15 July 1975.

microtechnology. The Soviets, clearly incapable of matching such expertise, seemed to have lost the race.

There is evidence that this was recognised by the Soviets before 1969, for they never really tried to carry out the extraordinarily complex business of placing their cosmonauts on other planets. Instead, they went for the Soyuz programme of creating and maintaining a space station, permanently orbiting the Earth under the command of replacement crews, the first of which took up its post in April 1971.

The Americans followed suit in May 1973 with the Skylab experiments and, in one brief moment of superpower collaboration, Soviet and American crews actually linked up in space, but this was rare. For most of the time, the rivalry persisted. In December 1970, for example, the Soviets landed an unmanned probe on Venus, triggering a similar American experiment on Mars six years later.

The Space Shuttle

As with the Moon programme, it was American money and expertise that forged ahead. By the early 1980s, scientists at NASA (National Aeronautical and Space Agency) had perfected a re-useable launch vehicle known as the Space Shuttle. This was actually a huge aircraft, launched into space by means of a vertical rocket, which could re-enter the Earth's atmosphere and land on a normal runway, ready for use again after appropriate servicing. Unfortunately, in January 1986, disaster struck the Shuttle programme when one of the vehicles blew up soon after launch, killing all seven astronauts on board. For a time, all American experiments ceased.

This is important not just in terms of prestige, but also because the space programme as a whole is now tied firmly to military needs. Both sides, for example, have launched enormous numbers of satellites since the late 1950s, and it is estimated that as many as 75 per cent of these have been for military use, providing the eyes and ears of the superpowers in space.

More importantly for the Americans in 1986, the Shuttle was an integral part of their Strategic Defense Initiative for the creation of "killer satellites". These are to be armed with laser or charged-particle weapons to destroy incoming Soviet ICBMs and depend heavily upon the Shuttle to carry supplies of fuel as well as parts of the satellites themselves.

As the Soviets seem to be striving to create their own Star Wars weapons, such an American setback could be crucial. The Space Race has probably only just entered its second round, with no definite winner yet in sight.

The Strategic Defense Initiative (Star Wars): as soon as Soviet ICBMs are launched (**1**), American "killer satellites" (**2**) use laser-beam weapons (**3**), to destroy them or their warheads (**4**). Any warheads that escape (**5**) are taken out by ground-based ABMs (anti-ballistic missiles) (**6**). To be effective, the system has to be "leak-proof", with no warheads getting through, but high cost and futuristic technology raise doubts about Star Wars becoming a reality before the year 2000.

CHRONOLOGY

1945

4-11 February Yalta Conference – Stalin, Churchill and Roosevelt discuss the post-war settlement

26 June United Nations Charter signed in San Francisco

16 July First US atomic bomb test, Alamogordo, New Mexico

16 July-2 August Potsdam Conference – Stalin, Attlee and Truman discuss Allied control of Germany

1946

5 March Churchill's "Iron Curtain" speech at Fulton, Missouri

1947

19 January Communist government "elected" in Poland

10 February Allies sign peace treaties with Italy, Romania, Bulgaria, Finland and Hungary

4 March Treaty of Dunkirk (Britain and France)

12 March Truman Doctrine announced, pledging US aid to countries fighting communist pressure

5 June Marshall Aid announced, offering US economic support to Europe (rejected by the Soviets, 12 July)

31 August Communists gain power in Hungary

1948

27 February Communist takeover in Czechoslovakia

13 March Treaty of Brussels

24 June Soviets impose road and rail blockade on West Berlin

1949

18 January Comecon created

4 April NATO formed

12 May Soviet blockade of West Berlin ends

23 May Federal Republic of Germany (West Germany) created

14 July Soviets test-explode their first atomic bomb

30 September Berlin airlift ends

7 October German Democratic Republic (East Germany) created

1950

25 June North Korean forces invade South Korea; US troops committed to defence of South Korea

1952

18 February Greece and Turkey join NATO

3 October First British atomic bomb test

1 November First US hydrogen bomb test

1953

5 March Death of Stalin; replaced by "collective leadership"

16-17 June Anti-communist riots in East Germany; suppressed by Soviet Army

12 August First Soviet hydrogen bomb test

1954

8 September South East Asia Treaty Organisation (SEATO) formed as part of "containment" of communism by the West

1955

24 February Baghdad Pact formed as part of "containment" of communism by the West (becomes the Central Treaty Organisation, August 1959)

5 May West Germany becomes a member of NATO

14 May Warsaw Pact formed

15 May Austrian State Treaty – Allied occupation ends, Austria becomes neutral

1956

28-29 June Popular rising in Poland, suppressed with Soviet military aid

23 October-4 November Crisis in Hungary ends with Soviet invasion

1957

25 March Treaty of Rome creates the European Economic Community (EEC); effective from 1 January 1958

4 October Soviet Union launches Sputnik I, the first artificial satellite

1958

27 March Nikita Khrushchev assumes sole leadership of the Soviet Union

1960

13 February First French atomic bomb test

1 May US pilot Gary Powers shot down in U-2 spy plane over the Soviet Union

16-17 May Paris Summit between Khrushchev and Eisenhower fails because of U-2 incident

8 November Kennedy elected US President

1961

17 April   CIA-backed invasion of Cuba (Bay of Pigs) fails

3-4 June   Vienna Summit between Khrushchev and Kennedy

12-13 August   Berlin Wall built

19 December   Albania breaks off diplomatic links with the Soviet Union (leaves the Warsaw Pact, 1968)

1962

16-28 October   Cuban Missile Crisis

1963

20 June   Hot-Line Agreement between US and Soviet Union to provide communications in time of crisis

25 July   Nuclear Test Ban Treaty

22 November   Kennedy assassinated

1964

15 October   Khrushchev dismissed from office, replaced by Brezhnev

20 October   First Chinese atomic bomb test

1966

7 March   France withdraws from the military structure of NATO

1968

1 July   Non-Proliferation Treaty

3-30 May   Student disturbances and worker's strike in Paris

20 August   Warsaw Pact invasion of Czechoslovakia to stop the implementation of "liberal" reforms

5 November   Richard Nixon elected US President

12 November   Brezhnev Doctrine announced

1969

17 November   Strategic Arms Limitation Talks (SALT) begin in Helsinki

1970

12 August   West Germany and the Soviet Union sign treaties guaranteeing frontiers

15-20 December   Civil disorder in Poland

1972

22 May   Moscow Summit – Nixon and Brezhnev sign SALT I

21 December   Treaty between East and West Germany, recognising each other's sovereignty

1973

30 October   Mutual and Balanced Force Reduction (MBFR) talks open in Vienna

1974

3 July   Moscow Summit – Nixon and Brezhnev sign Threshold Test-Ban Treaty

20 July   Turkish invasion of Cyprus

8 August   Nixon resigns as US President over the Watergate affair; replaced by Ford

23 November   Vladivostok Summit – Ford and Brezhnev agree "ceiling" figures for nuclear arms

1975

1 August   Helsinki Accords

1979

18 May   Vienna Summit – Carter and Brezhnev sign SALT II

4 November   Iranian students seize US embassy in Tehran

26 December   Soviet forces invade Afghanistan

1980

24-25 April   Operation Eagle Claw – US rescue attempt of hostages in Tehran – fails

1-31 August   Widespread disturbances in Poland, led by the trade union Solidarity

4 November   Reagan elected US President

1981

30 November.   Intermediate Nuclear Force (INF) talks begin in Geneva (end without agreement, December 1983)

13 December   Martial law declared in Poland

1982

30 May   Spain becomes 16th member of NATO

29 June   Strategic Arms Reduction Talks (START) begin in Geneva

1983

23 March   Reagan announces his Strategic Defense Initiative plan

25 October   US troops invade Grenada

14 November   First US Cruise missiles arrive in Britain

1985

17 March   Gorbachev becomes Soviet leader

19-21 November   Geneva Summit – Reagan and Gorbachev meet to discuss arms control

1986

11 October   Reagan and Gorbachev meet at Reykjavik; fail to achieve agreement

INDEX

Note: Numbers in bold refer to illustrations or maps

Abel, Rudolf Ivanovich, 55
ABM, 26, 27, 40
Adenaur, Konrad, 23
Afghanistan, 31-32, **32**, 35, **47**, 51
Alamogordo, 36
Albania, 10, 15, 43, 46
alliances, 42-47
Allies, 6-7, 8, 12-13, 15, 50
Andropov, Yuri, 35
Angola, 30, **30**
anti-ballistic missiles, see ABM
Anti-Ballistic Missile Treaty, 27
Arabian Gulf, see Persian Gulf
Argentina, 26, 40
arms control, 26-27, 34-35
Armstrong, Neil, 56
atomic weapons, see nuclear capability
Attlee, Prime Minister Clement, 8
Australia, 15
Austria, 8, 10, 15, 45
Austrian State Treaty, 15, 18, 43

B-1B bomber, 39, 53
B-52 bomber, 39, 53
Backfire bomber, see Tupolev Tu-26
Baghdad Pact, 15
Batista, Fulgencio, 19
Bay of Pigs, 20
Belgium, 13, 23, 33, 43, 50
Berlin; 50; division of city, 8, 23; blockade and airlift, 12-13, 25, 43; Berlin wall, 18-19, **19**, 25, 39
Berlin Wall, 18-19, **18**
Blackjack bomber, 34
Blake, George, 55
Blunt, Anthony, 55
Boeing AGM-86B ALCM missile, **28**
Brandenburg Gate, **18**
Brandt, Willy, 23
Brazil, 26
Brezhnev, Leonid, 25, 27, **27**, 48, **48**
Brezhnev Doctrine, 25, 35
brinkmanship, 20-21, 25
Broz Josip, see Tito
Brussels, Treaty of, 13, 43
Budapest, **16**
buffer zones, 7-8, 9, 27, 43
Bulgaria, 10, 15, 43, 46
Burgess, Guy, 55

Cambodia, 29
Canada, 13, 27, 43, 50
capability, 37, 38
Caribbean, 34-35, 51
Carter, President Jimmy, 28, 29, 31, 32, 48
Castro, Fidel, 19-21, 51
CENTO, 15
Central America, 33-35, 51
Central Intelligence Agency, see CIA
Central Treaty Organisation, see CENTO
Chernenko, Konstantin, 35
China, 10, 14, 25, 37
China card, 25, 32
Churchill, Prime Minister Winston, 7-8, 48
CIA, 20, 54-55
Cold War, 8-9
Comecon, 11
Cominform, 11
Common Market, see EEC
communications, 37, 38
communism, 9
Communist Information Bureau, see Cominform
Conference on Security and Co-operation in Europe, see CSCE
Confidence Building Measures (CBMs), 27
containment, 10, 14-15
Contras, 34
Control Council, 8
conventional forces, 37, 46, 52-53
cost-gain calculation, 37
Council for Mutual Economic Assistance, see Comecon
credibility, 37, 38
crisis management, 26
cruise missiles, 29, **35**
CSCE, 27, **27**, 28
Cuba, 19-21, 25, 26, 29, 33, 34, 35
Cuban Missile Crisis, 19-21, 22, 35, 39
Cyprus, 43, 45
Czechoslovakia, 10, 11, **11**, 15, 24-25, 26, 33, 43, 46

de Gaulle, Charles, 23
denazification, 6-7
Denmark, 13, 23, 43
detente, 22-23, 25-32, 33
deterrence, 37-41, 45-47, 53
Diego Garcia, 33
Dubček, Alexander, 24-25, **24**, 48
Dulles, John Foster, 15, 38
Dunkirk, Treaty of, 13, 42
Dwight D. Eisenhower, USS, **54**

Eastern Europe, 9, 10-12, 16-17, 27, 43-47
East Germany, see German Democratic Republic

EEC, 23
Egypt, 17, 32, 33
Eisenhower, President Dwight D., 15, 17, 20
El Salvador, 34, 51, **51**
Emerging Technology, 47
Ethiopia, 30
European Economic Community, see EEC

Falklands War, 52
fascism, see Nazi Party
first strike, 39, 40
fission bombs, 36
flashpoints, 50-51
flexible response, 46
Florida, 20, 21
FOFA, 52
Ford, President Gerald, 27
France: Marshall Plan, 10; Berlin, 12; and NATO, 13, 15, 42, 43, 45; Indochina, 14; EEC, 23; nuclear capability, 37, 45
Fuchs, Dr Klaus, 14, 55, **55**
fusion bombs, 36

Gagarin, Yuri, 56, **56**
Gdansk, 33
German Democratic Republic, 13, 15, 16, 18-19, 23, 43
German Federal Republic, 13, 15, 23, 33, 43, 45, 50, 51
Germany; post-war settlement, 6-8, 10; Berlin blockade, 12-13
Glenn, John, 56
Goering, Hermann, 7, **7**
Golitsyn, Anatoli, 55
Gomulka, Wladyslaw, 17
Gorbachev, Mikhail, 35, 48, **48**
Gorshkov, Sergei, 48
Gouzenko, Igor, 55
Government Communications Headquarters (GCHQ), 54
graduated deterrence, 39, 45, 50
Greece, 10, 15, 23, 43, 45
Greenham Common, 33, **35**, 53
Grenada, 34, 51
ground-launched cruise missiles (GLCMs), 33, 34, 53, **53**
Group of Soviet Forces Germany, 50

Havana, 19, 21
Helsinki, 26, **27**
Helsinki Accords, 27
Hess, Rudolf, 7
Hiroshima, 36, **37**, 38
Hitler, Adolf, 6
Hot-Line Agreement, 22, **23**, 26
Houghton, Harry, 55
human error, 41
human rights, 27
Hungary, 10, 15, 16-17, **16**, 25, 33, 43, 46
Husak, Gustav, 25

ICBM, 17, 21, 23, 27, 34, 39, **39**, 40, 41, 53, 57
Iceland, 13, 43
IGB, 44, 45, 50
India, 26
Inner-German Border, see IGB
intercontinental ballistic missiles, see ICBM
Intermediate-Range Nuclear Force talks (INF), 34
Iran, 15, **30**, 31, 41, 51
Iraq, 15, 40, 51
Ireland, 23
Iron Curtain, 11
Israel, 26, 40, 51
Italy, 10, 13, 21, 23, 33, 43, 45

Japan, 7, 8
Jaruzelski, General Wojciech, 33
Johnson, President Lyndon B., 19, 23, 25, 29

Kabul, 31
Kadar, Janos 17
Karmal, Babrak, 31
Kennedy, President John F., 17, 18-21, 22, 23, 49, **49**, 56
Kenya, 33
KGB, 54-55
Khomeini, Ayatollah, **30**, 31, 41
Khrushchev, Premier Nikita, 15, 17, 18-21, 25, 49
Kommandatura, 12, 50
Korean War, 14, 21, 38, 51
Kroger, Peter and Helen, 55

Laika, 17
Laos, 29
laser-beam weapons, 40
Latin America, 19-21, 26, 33-35, 51
Liberty, USS, 26
Lonsdale, Gordon, 55
Luxembourg, 13, 23, 43

Maclean, Donald, 55
McCarthy, Senator Joseph, 14, **14**
McNamara, Robert, 39
MAD, 39-40, 41
Malaya, 14
Malmedy, 7
Manhattan Project, 36
Mao Tse-tung, 10, 14
Marshall, General George, 10
Marshall Plan, 10, **11**, 11
Marucla, 21
Masaryk, Jan, 11
massive retaliation, 38-39, 45
May, Dr Allen Nunn, 54, 55
MI6, 54
Minuteman III ICBM, **40**
MIRVs, 28, 40
missile gap, 17
Morocco, 33
mujaheddin, 32, **32**
multiple independently

targeted re-entry vehicle, *see*
    MIRV
multiple re-entry vehicles
    (MRVs) 27, 28
Mutual and Balanced Force
    Reduction Talks (MBFR), 27
mutual assured destruction,
    see MAD
MX Peacekeeper, 34

Nagasaki, 38
Nagy, Imre, 16-17
NASA, 57
Nationalist Chinese, 10, 14
NATO; creation of, 13, **13**, 14,
    15, 16, 42-43, **43**, 45; arms
    control, 27, 33; strategic
    position, 38, 45-46; 50-51,
    52-53
naval forces, 52
Navy Ring, 55
Nazi Party, 6-7, **7**
Netherlands, 13, 23, 33, 43, 50
New Zealand, 15
Nicaragua, 34, 51
Nixon, President Richard, 25,
    27, 49, **49**, 56
Non-Proliferation Treaty, 26
North Atlantic Treaty
    Organisation, *see* NATO
North Korea, 14
Norway, 13, 43, 44, 45
Novotny, Antonin, 24
nuclear bombs, 36-37
nuclear capability, 9, 14, 17,
    20-21, 23, 26, 36-41, 52-53
nuclear mines, 26
nuclear parity, 23, 26
nuclear proliferation, 26
Nuclear Test-Ban Treaty, 26
nuclear testing, 26, 35
nuclear umbrella, 45-46
Nuremberg Trials, 7, **7**

Ohio class, 34
Olympic Games, 31
Oman, 33
Operation Eagle Claw, 31
Operation Urgent Fury, 34
Organisation of American
    States, 14
Ostpolitik, 23
Outer Space Treaty, 26

Pakistan, 15, 26, 40
Panama Canal, 33, 51
Panjsher Valley, **32**
Paris summit (1959), 17
peaceful co-existence, 15
peace movements, 34-35, **35**
Penkovsky, Oleg, 55
Pershing II missiles, 33
Persian Gulf, 31-33, 51
Philby, Kim, 55
Philippines, 14, 15
Poland, 7-8, 10, 15, 23, 33, 43,
    46
Polaris missiles, **37**
Portugal, 13, 23, 43, 45

Potsdam Conference, 8, 15
Powers, Gary, 17, 20, 54
Prague, **24**, 25
Prague Spring, 25
proliferation, 26

Quadripartite Agreement, 23

Radio Free Europe, 14
Rakosi, Matyas, 16
Rapid Deployment Joint Task
    Force (RDJTF), 33
rationality, 37, 38, 41
Reagan, President Ronald, 29,
    31, 34, 35, 40, 49, **49**, 53
reparations, 8
Romania, 10, 15, 43
Rome, Treaty of, 23
Roosevelt, President Franklin
    D., 7-8
Rosenberg, Julius and Ethel,
    14, 55, **55**
Rusk, Dean, 21

SALT; Salt I, 26-27, 28; SALT
    II, 28-29, 33; SALT III, 29
Sam Rayburn, USS, **37**
Sandinistas, 34, 51
satellites, 54-57
satellite states, 11, 43
Saudi Arabia, 32
SDI, 35, 40, 53, 57
Seabed Treaty, 26
SEATO, 15
Second World War, 6, 15
Secret Intelligence Service
    (SIS), 54, 55
Shepard, Alan, 56
Shuttle programme, 57
Six-Day War, 26
Skylab programme, 57
SLBM, 23, 39, 40, 53
Solidarity, 33
Somalia, 33
Somoza, General Anastasio, 34
South Africa, 26, 30, 40
South East Asia Treaty
    Organisation, *see* SEATO
South Korea, 14
Soviet Union; post-war
    settlement, 7-8; political
    system, 8-9; Berlin, 12-13,
    18-19; and Warsaw Pact, 15,
    43-47, 50; Hungary, 16-17;
    nuclear capability, 17, 23,
    34-35, 37-41; Cuba, 19-21;
    Czechoslovakia, 24-25;
    detente, 25-32; arms control
    agreements, 26-29, 34-35;
    and Third World, 29-31;
    Afghanistan, 31-32
Soyuz programme, 57
space-based weapons, 40-41,
    56-57
space race, 56-57
Spain, 23, 43, 45
Sputnik satellites, 17, 56
spying, 54-55
SR-71 Blackbird, 54

SS-20 missiles, 33, 34, 53
Stalin, Marshal Josef; Yalta,
    7-8; origins of Cold War, 9;
    soviet expansion, 10-11;
    Berlin blockade, 12-13;
Star Wars, 35
Strategic Arms Limitation
    Talks, *see* SALT
Strategic Arms Reduction
    Talks (START), 34
Strategic Defense Initiative,
    see SDI
strategic nuclear launchers, 27
submarine-launched ballistic
    missiles, *see* SLBM
superpowers, 15, 23
Switzerland, 45

technology, nuclear, 39-41
Tehran embassy crisis, 31
Tereshkova, Valentina, 56
Tet Offensive, 29
Thailand, 15
theatre weapons, 33, 53
Threshold Test-Ban Treaty, 27
Tito, 11, 51
Tomahawk GLCM, **53**
Truman, President Harry S, 8,
    10-12, 15, 49
Truman Doctrine, 10
Tupolev Tu-26 "Backfire"
    bomber, 28, **28**, 29, 53
Turkey, 10, 15, 21, 43, 45

U-2 reconnaissance planes, 17,
    20, 21, 54
Un-American Activities
    subcommittee, 14, **14**
United Kingdom; post-war
    settlement, 6-8; and Greece,
    10; Berlin airlift, 12-13;
    NATO, 13, 15, 42, 43, 50;
    Malaya, 14; nuclear
    weapons, 21, 33, 37
United Nations, 14, 17, 23, 31
United States; post-war
    settlement, 6-8; political
    system, 8-9; and Soviet
    expansion, 10; Berlin, 12-13,
    18-19; NATO, 13, 14-15,
    43-47, 50-51; nuclear
    capability, 17, 23, 34-35,
    37-41; Cuba, 19-21; detente,
    25-32; arms control
    agreements, 26-29, 34-35;
    weakness, 29-31
Ussuri River, 25

Vienna, 8
Vienna summit (1961), 17, 20
Viet Cong, 29
Vietnam War, 25, 29, 32, 34,
    45
Vladivostok, 27, 28
Voice of America, 14

Walesa, Lech, 33, 49, **49**
Walker spy ring, 55
Warsaw Pact; creation of, 15,

43; Hungary, 16-17, 24, 25;
    arms control, 27; strategic
    position, 45-47, 50-51, 52-53
Watergate, 29
West Berlin, *see* Berlin
Western Allies, *see* Allies
West Germany, *see* German
    Federal Republic

Yalta Conference, 7-8, **8**
Yugoslavia, 10, 11, 51

Zaire, 30

GLOSSARY OF TERMS

Arms Control agreements to limit the numbers and types of weapons (usually nuclear) deployed by East and West.

Arms Race the development of weapons systems by both superpowers, designed to prevent the opposition gaining an advantage.

Cold War the state of mistrust and hostility between East and West, stopping short of military action. Usually applied to the period 1945-62.

Crisis Management actions taken by the superpowers to prevent minor incidents blowing up into major confrontations.

Detente an easing of tensions between East and West, usually applied to the period 1963-79.

Deterrence actions and threats designed to prevent aggression by persuading a potential opponent that any such move on his part would be too costly (usually used in a nuclear context, in which the threat of nuclear attack is implied).

Disarmament the physical removal or dismantling of weapons.

Flexible Response a NATO strategy, adopted in 1967, in which any Warsaw Pact aggression will be met.

Limited War conscious restraint on the use of force in the event of war, usually in terms of weapons (especially nuclear), targets and numbers.

MAD (Mutual Assured Destruction) a situation in which any nuclear attack by one side can be absorbed and sufficient forces remain to carry out a devastating retaliatory response.

Massive Retaliation US strategy, adopted in 1954, whereby any attack on the West would be met with instant nuclear response. Phased out, early 1960s.

New Cold War the period of renewed tension between the superpowers since the late 1970s.

Star Wars journalistic term for President Reagan's Strategic Defense Initiative (SDI), announced in March 1983: a plan for the creation of space-based defence against Soviet missiles aimed at the United States.

Superpower title given to countries of immense power, military strength (notably nuclear) and influence: currently the United States and Soviet Union only, although Communist China has the potential to join them.

FURTHER READING

Abel, E. *The Missiles of October* (Macgibbon and Kee, 1969)

Ash, T.G. *The Polish Revolution* (Jonathan Cape, 1983)

Baylis, J., Booth, K., Garnett, J., and Williams, P. *Contemporary Strategy* (Croom Helm, 1975)

Bidwell, Brig. S. *World War III* (Hamlyn, 1978)

Bonds, R. (ed) *The Soviet War Machine* (Salamander, 1980)

Calder, N. *Nuclear Nightmares* (Penguin, 1981)

Calvocoressi, P. *World Politics Since 1945* (Longman, 1977)

Campbell, C. *War Facts Now* (Fontana, 1982)

Detzer, D. *The Brink: The Cuban Missile Crisis of 1962* (Dent, 1980)

Edmonds, R. *Soviet Foreign Policy. The Brezhnev Years* (Oxford University Press, 1983)

Freedman, L. *Atlas of Global Strategy* (Macmillan, 1985)

Fullerton, J. *The Soviet Occupation of Afghanistan* (Methuen, 1984)

Hackett, Gen. Sir J. (ed) *The Third World War* (Sidgwick and Jackson, 1978)

Henderson, Sir N. *The Birth of NATO* (Weidenfeld and Nicolson, 1982)

International Institute for Strategic Studies: 'Military Balance' and 'Strategic Survey' (annual publications)

Morgan, R. *The Unsettled Peace. A Study of the Cold War in Europe* (BBC Publications, 1974)

Morris, E. *Blockade. Berlin and the Cold War* (Hamish Hamilton, 1973)

Pringle, P. and Arkin, W. *SIOP. Nuclear War from the Inside* (Sphere, 1983)

Remington, R. A. *The Warsaw Pact* (MIT Press, Cambridge, Mass., 1971)

Suvorov, V. *Inside the Soviet Army* (Hamilton, 1982)

Thompson, E. P. (ed) *Star Wars* (Penguin, 1985)

Thompson, Sir R. *War in Peace* (Orbis, 1985)

War in Peace Partwork (Orbis, 1983-85)

Wilson, A. *The Disarmers' Handbook of Military Technology* (Penguin, 1983)

(NOTE: All publishers located in London unless specified otherwise)